Around the World
in a
Bad Mood!

Around the World
in a
Bad Mood!

Confessions
of a Flight Attendant

Rene Foss

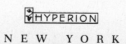

NEW YORK

Library of Congress Cataloging-in-Publication Data

Foss, Rene.
    Around the world in a bad mood : confessions of a flight attendant / Rene Foss.
        p. cm.
    ISBN: 0-7868-9011-8
    1. Flight attendants. 2. Foss, Rene, 1962– I. Title.

HD8039.A43 R67 2002
387.7'42'092—dc21
[B]   2001039884

FIRST EDITION

10   9   8   7   6   5   4   3   2   1

Book design by Lynne Amft

This book is dedicated to my parents,

Robert and Maxyne,

with love

Around the World
in a
Bad Mood!

Introduction

I AM A FLIGHT ATTENDANT and the world is my oyster. And what an oyster it is! Oversold flights, weather delays, air traffic control delays, center seats, crappy food, air rage—it's so glamorous! Kind of like a Greyhound bus in the sky.

Recently I have been wondering: Perhaps I made the wrong career choice? There I was on my last layover, curled up in the fetal position on the bathroom floor of a Motel 6 in downtown Flint. I said aloud to my bottle of Jack Daniel's, "Jack, what will ever become of me? Am I destined to push a meal cart up and down an aisle for the rest of my days? Politely telling people— who are so crammed into their seats that major portions of their bodies are spilled over the armrests—to watch their elbows, feet, and other assorted body parts? And asking if they would like chicken or beef? When I'm seventy-five will I still be hiding behind a fake smile (if I have any teeth left, that is), breathing recycled air, demonstrating to the suffering sea of humanity how to operate a seat belt? Oh Jack, this is not what I had in mind. Where did I make the wrong turn that led me here?"

This was not an easy question to answer. I have made a lot of wrong turns in my life. I had to think this through. Fortunately for me, time was on my side: What else is there to do in downtown Flint on a fifty-four-hour layover, but think about your pain? I'd already been to Denny's. So I removed the noose from my neck and I began to think. Why not tell the people of the world, most of whom are probably in bad moods of their own, about my bad mood, and my journey thus far? So here's a story about air travel, flight attendants, and me! Fasten your seat belts, raise your tray table, and stow your bag. . . . The journey is about to begin.

Welcome to my nightmare!

Father Knows Best

YOU MIGHT BE WONDERING why I became a flight attendant in the first place. I ask myself that very question every day. A lot of people think that because my mother was a "stewardess" for eight years in the golden age of air travel, the 1950s, that I chose the flight attendant profession to follow in her footsteps. Not true. Frankly, I had no interest in the airline industry whatsoever. I had other things in mind: SHOW BUSINESS! I can't remember ever wanting to do anything else but be in show biz, preferably in front of the camera or an audience. And starring roles only, please. I loved to be the center of attention, to sing and dance, and to dramatize everything that happened. People have told me throughout my entire life that I have an overactive imagination and should try to put it to positive use. Show business was the natural choice, a logical progression, and there was no one who could tell me otherwise. I wanted to be a star, and once I make up my mind about something, it is pretty difficult to sway me. Of course, there were naysayers. The ones who tried to deter me, to discourage me, to stop me. Ha! Let 'em try, I had it all planned. I was going to take classes, read plays, get head shots, and make contacts. Then I was going to New York City to suffer for my art, and after a fair amount of suffering, someone would discover my natural ability and send me off to Hollywood, where I'd be in pictures and make oodles of cash. What plans I had! And I wasn't that far off, either. After all, I was playing the jumping mouse (the lead!) in my high school play.

It went on like this throughout high school and college, and looking back on my youthful aspirations I'll be the first to admit that my enthusiasm was incommensurate with my actual theatrical talents. But when you're twenty-two, with a heart full of hope, there is very little that can stand in your way. Except maybe your dad.

My dad, Bob, thought it was charming that I was so interested in the theater until he began to realize that I was serious. Then he began to rein me in. I was living at home, waiting tables, and going to auditions for theaters that didn't pay. This was not acceptable for a college graduate. It was time to get serious, grow up, and get a job with *benefits*! Starting immediately after graduation, my father took every opportunity to speak about the joys of gainful employment.

BOB: Say, I heard Susie Smith from your high school class just started working for IBM.

RENE: Oh, that's nice. What is she doing?

BOB: She's a secretary to one of the big shots over there.

RENE: The last thing I would want to do every day is work nine to five in an office.

BOB: But she's making good money and she has terrific *benefits*! She's also moving into her very own apartment.

RENE: Dad, how many times do I have to remind you? I'm going to New York City to work in the *theater*. . . .

BOB: Rene, how many times do I have remind you that no daughter of mine is going to New York City to work in the *theater*. Got it?

At that point I would change the subject or leave the room. His mission to rein me in was not confined to our private conversations. No way. I can remember one time he attended a play in which I performed at a very fine, well-established local theater. I had a central role, but no actual lines. Believe it or not, the play was well received—and so was I. In the lobby after one performance, people were congratulating me and saying hello. I was there with my father who, despite his aversion to my career choice, was secretly beaming about my small success. A family friend approached.

FAMILY FRIEND: Oh Rene, it was wonderful! You did such a fine job. I couldn't take my eyes off you—what presence you have onstage! Bob, wasn't she wonderful? What did you think?

BOB: I couldn't believe she could keep her mouth shut for ninety minutes. You know acting is a risky thing, and not very steady. I think Rene should keep it as a hobby—like golf—and start concentrating on finding a job with *benefits*.

I was getting tired of hearing about *benefits,* but I was living at home (his home) and he had a point about not being paid for the work you do. I was also getting tired of waiting tables (although I was an excellent waitress, and was one of the best at the restaurant). But mostly, I was getting tired of being at odds with my dad. We had always been so close and had a lot of fun together, and I missed that. So in order to keep peace in the family, I began the job interview process. When you want to be an actress, it's difficult to sell yourself to a brokerage firm, a communications company, or a commodities corporation. Needless to say, I wasn't getting very far. Then one day my dad (we were friends again now that I was selling my soul to corporate

America) burst into the house after work with a newspaper in his hands:

BOB: Rene, the airlines are having open interviews this week. You can go over to the airport and pick up an application!
RENE: An application for what?
BOB (smiling): To be a stewardess.
RENE: I think they're called flight attendants these days, Dad.

I reluctantly took the newspaper as he handed it to me and read the ad:

ARE YOU LOOKING FOR A CAREER THAT IS EXCITING AND GLAMOROUS? DO YOU LIKE TO TRAVEL AND WORK WITH THE PUBLIC? WE ARE SEEKING CANDIDATES WHO ARE PROFESSIONAL, POISED, AND SERVICE-MINDED FOR IMMEDIATE OPENINGS AS FLIGHT ATTENDANTS. CANDIDATES MUST BE WILLING TO RELOCATE TO ANY OF OUR BASES: NEW YORK, CHICAGO, SAN FRANCISCO.

After I saw the words "New York" things started going in slow motion. It began to make sense that I would become a flight attendant. I would go to the New York base, find an apartment, make some money, travel around for about six months, and then quit the airline to pursue that acting career.

RENE: What a great idea, Dad! I love it, and I'm sure they would take me. They'd be lucky to have me! I mean, I *am* one of the best waitresses at the restaurant—the customers love me.

A look of surprise came across my dad's face at this point. I guess he was expecting a smart-ass comment instead of enthusiasm.

BOB: That's right, you're perfect for the job! The pay is great and so are the *benefits*. But more important, your mother flew for eight years so be sure to mention that in the interview. Also be sure to ask about medical insurance and the retirement package . . . blah, blah, blah.

The sound of his voice began to fade and I could hear only music in my head, like the soundtrack to a film at a very dramatic moment in the story. I had a feeling this was one of those defining moments in life. My dad was happy, and I was actually getting excited about this idea of becoming a flight attendant. All those travel benefits! I wouldn't mind taking a few trips to see the world, but most of all, this was my ticket to New York City. That was it: The next thing I knew I was off to the airport to pick up my application to become a flight attendant. Not exactly my first choice of a dream job, but how bad could it be?

Love People, Love to Travel
The Interview

EVEN THOUGH THE LIFESTYLE, free travel, and possibility of living in New York appealed to me, prior to Feb-
ruary 20, 1985, I had given very little thought to the
actual job of being a flight attendant. It was just another day, and
another interview. But as soon as I walked into the waiting room
at "We Apologize for This Inconvenience Airlines" (WAFTI) and
saw the other candidates wearing crisp blue suits, perfectly
coiffed hairdos, and phony smiles, it quickly became apparent
that this was unlike any other job interview I'd ever been on. It
was more like a cross between an audition for a major motion
picture and a beauty pageant. Everyone looked so perky, so
attractive, and so approachable, but behind those painted smiles
and cemented bobs, I could sense that none of the candidates
would mind too much if I fell backward down a flight of stairs.
That would automatically disqualify one from the job, and thus
increase the others' chances of getting that strangely coveted
career of "flight attendant."

At once my competitive streak kicked in. Seeing how much
everyone else seemed to desire this position made me want it
also. I hadn't wanted it when I woke up that morning, but now it
was as though I *had* to be selected: I was going to be a flight
attendant or die! I had had a lot more confidence when I didn't
want the job. Now that I found myself actually wanting it, my

confidence began to falter: "What if they don't pick me? How humiliating to be turned down by WAFTI. Everyone else is so put together and so tall. They probably won't pick me. . . . I should have written neater on the application. . . . I should have worn a different suit. . . . God, I hope I get it. . . . I really need this job."

Just as I was about to burst into my own rendition of "A Chorus Line," a tall, officious blond woman with red nail polish called us into a small fluorescent-lit room and asked us, or rather told us, to have seat. The chairs were in a semicircle and there were no windows in the room. It was warm and I began to feel as though there were not enough oxygen in the room. We sat down in the order in which we had entered. Facing us were two other women and a man, all of whom had that steely, efficient, crisp demeanor that personifies the term "professional." They took turns talking about how the interview process would work and what we could expect in the event we were "invited" (as in "invited to a party," but this had no resemblance to a party) into a training class. One got the distinct feeling WAFTI did not need you, but you needed WAFTI and you were just damn lucky to have the opportunity to meet them and simply set foot on the premises.

The officious blonde spoke, "You must be willing to work nights, weekends, and holidays. If you are selected you will attend a seven-week unpaid training program and will be required to live in the company-arranged housing for training candidates. You must be willing to relocate to any of our bases throughout the United States; unfortunately, we do not know where we need you, so we will not be able to tell you where you will be based until the final day of the training, should you make it that far. We will, however, give you a one-way ticket to your new base. You are required to purchase your uniform, which must be properly maintained in accordance with company standards at all times. The cost is seven hundred dollars. We do realize that you will probably not have this sort of money when and if you complete the *unpaid* training, so we will give you the uniform and payroll will deduct the cost from your paycheck until it is paid in full. When you start out with WAFTI you will be on reserve status—that is to say that you must be available twenty-two days out of each month for a trip assignment. We will always give you as much notice as possible, but since "reserves" fill in for flight attendants who have called in sick or cannot make it to their flight for some reason, sometimes you'll have very short notice—maybe as little as an hour. We expect that you will be prepared and able to get to work in this allotted time period. After all, WAFTI will be counting on you, as will our passengers. We cannot stress the importance of your dependability when you are on reserve, therefore we have put certain regulations in place to ensure that you are available for an assignment. First of all, central scheduling will contact you by phone, so you must have a telephone at your contact residence, which must be within a one-hour radius of the airport. Second, you are not allowed to have a beeper or pager; we expect that you will be home by the phone with your bag packed and your uniform cleaned, waiting. This seems harsh, but everyone has put their time in on reserve and eventually you will have enough seniority to hold a set schedule."

What she failed to mention is that when you finally do get off reserve—after about four years—and you begin holding a set schedule, it will be a schedule that no one else in their right mind would want: six legs a day, followed by a ten-hour layover in a fleabag motel about two hundred feet off the runway in some dismal, dirty, depressed city. And thanks to the length of your layover (or rather lack of it) and the fact that it will be dark the entire time, you will not have the misfortune of actually seeing your surroundings. However, after years on reserve you will welcome the predictability of these horrid schedules and the fact that you no longer have to be tethered to the telephone, waiting for a call that comes at 2:00 A.M. informing you that you are going to Buffalo at 5:00 A.M.! Yes, the day a flight attendant is finally freed from the shackles of reserve she knows the true meaning of the word "liberation."

I was beginning to wonder about those *benefits*—so far it seemed as if there weren't too many—but before I had an opportunity to raise my hand the blonde informed us that it was time to introduce ourselves to the group. We were to go around the semicircle and stand up one by one to tell our names, where we were from, and why we wanted to be a flight attendant. This gave the WAFTI panel of experts an opportunity to evaluate our poise, our appearance, and whether we were intelligent enough to string a few words together and form a sentence. As each candidate stood and addressed the group, the panel was taking fast and furious notes. This was the part that was like an audition and it really didn't intimidate me too much, but what bothered me was the lack of originality in the responses of the candidates.

"I am Susie Glutz from the great state of Texas and I want to be a flight attendant because I just love people, I am very service-oriented, and I am a team player!" Followed by a big, fake smile.

"I am Yo' Vinnie, originally from New York, and I want to be a flight attendant because I love to travel and I want to see the world." Even bigger fake smile, but with missing teeth.

"I am Mary, Mary Quite Contrary from Kansas City, and I want to be a flight attendant because I just love people, I love to travel, *and* I love to smile." Big, big fake smile *and* batting eyelashes!

Had I known then what I know now I would have said: "My name is Rene and I am hoping to find a job that allows me to deal with emotionally and physically abusive passengers in a confined space. I am looking forward to spending a minimum of four years on reserve, having absolutely no life outside this job. But most important, I have a particular fondness for picking up trash, germs, disease, and other assorted garbage from hundreds of people from all over the planet and then saying 'thank you' with a big smile on my face! I feel I am qualified because I have the ability to converse with utter strangers about meaningless subjects while I'm suffering from a headache, hangover, sleep deprivation, or jet lag. After working a ten-hour day I can eat my dinner—which often consists of leftover food that no one else wants—in five minutes or less, standing up in a galley filled with all the trash I just collected."

But what did I know back then? I was young and stupid, so I merely responded: "I'm Rene and I, too, love people and love to travel." Trouble with the fake smile.

It went on like this until everybody had their fifteen seconds of fame and then we were ushered back into the lobby to wait. I would have given anything to have been a fly on the wall in the conference room. There they dissected us while we were in the lobby, sweating it out while trying to look calm, approachable, and not too competitive. After thirty-five minutes they emerged and informed us that everyone would now be called in for a one-on-one interview. There was a collective straightening of the spine as the phony smiles immediately returned to the faces of weary candidates. I was hoping I would be called first, so I could get it over with and go have a cheeseburger. Of course, I was not first, or second, or even third. I was second to last. "Rene Foss!," called a voice. I looked up expecting the officious blonde, but was relieved to see a younger, mousy woman who had a very limp handshake. We walked down a corridor making idle chitchat about God-only-knows-what until we reached a dreary office. With my handwritten application in her hand, the interrogation began:

MOUSY LADY: Is this your present address?

RENE: Yes.

MOUSY LADY: Are you currently employed as a waitress at Hamburger Harry's?

RENE: Yes. I'm also currently performing in a play at . . .

MOUSY LADY: We'll get to that in a minute. I am required to verify certain information first. Now, have you ever been convicted of a crime, misdemeanor, or felony?

RENE: No, I don't think so.

MOUSY LADY: Well, you've stated on this application that you have not. Is that true? Or is there anything you need to tell me?

RENE: Yes.

MOUSY LADY: Yes? There is something you need to tell me?

RENE: No, yes, it is true! I mean, I haven't committed any crimes.

MOUSY LADY: Fine. Do you recognize this as your signature? And is everything on this application true?

RENE: Yes . . . to both.

It went on like that for quite some time. She would ask a question about why I wanted to be a flight attendant or how my current coworkers would describe me, and I'd enthusiastically respond, and then she would return my enthusiasm with a blank stare and move on to the next question.

MOUSY LADY: Are you willing to relocate?

RENE: Absolutely, I'd love to be based in New York or . . .

MOUSY LADY (interrupting): Are you willing to work nights, weekends, and holidays for the rest of your natural-born life?

RENE: Uhhh, yes, I guess.

MOUSY LADY: Good, now let me give you a mathematical problem. There are twelve people in first class, but only three meals. What would you do?

RENE: Gee, could that really happen?

MOUSY LADY: Yes, that's how we make a profit. What would you
    do?

RENE: Well, I guess I would serve the first three passengers the
    meals that were there and then tell the other nine passen-
    gers that they were shit out of luck and how sorry I am, and
    then I would hide in the bathroom the rest of the flight.

After twenty minutes I was fairly certain that I had blown it
big time. I was getting ready for that cheeseburger when she
informed me that she would like to send me over to the WAFTI
doctor for a pre-employment physical that would include (she
raised an eyebrow here) a drug test. (Damn, I knew I shouldn't
have visited that opium den last night with my friend Lou. He
promised me it would be out of my system within twenty-four
hours. . . . He better be right.) She said I should also be prepared
to provide them with my complete medical background. It was at
that point that I saw a glimmer of what resembled a smile.

MOUSY LADY: Very good. Oh, I almost forgot: Would you be will-
    ing to cut your hair?

RENE: Excuse me?

MOUSY LADY: Cut your hair. We have very strict grooming guide-
    lines and our appearance experts will be evaluating you early
    on in the training program. They make suggestions to the
    candidates about how they can improve their appearance
    and style to better fit in with the "company personality."

RENE: Gee, I guess I'd be willing to cut my hair. I mean if I'm
    going to be working nights, weekends, and holidays for the
    rest of my life, I guess it really doesn't matter what I look like!

MOUSY LADY: Very good, then it's off to the clinic for you.

I was only here to look for a job, to keep peace in my family, and to get some *benefits* and maybe get a few free trips. Now, in addition to all that, it seems I would be getting a new personality and a new hairdo. How fabulous! Well, no time to linger and ponder the new me, it was off to the clinic! I wondered if the doctor would be performing a lobotomy along with the drug test. Maybe he'd be doing my hair as well.

BENEFITS

I always thought I'd be a star.
(since she was two),
I'd drink champagne with caviar
(the ingénue).
Then my dad, Bob, said, "Get a job."
(boo-hoo-hoo-hoo)
"Get off the couch and get a job today!"
(forget the stage)

My dad said, "Try the airline,"
(you'll be a stew),
"the pay is good, they'll treat you fine"
(that's not so true)
"and you will learn to serve tidbits"
(what should she do?)
"you'll be so glad if a recession hits."

You'll have those BENEFITS.
A steady job that pays
BENEFITS, every year a big fat raise,

BENEFITS, strong earning potential, health
and life and dental . . . wake up girl, reality!

I breezed through that job interview.
(in a suit of blue)
They loved me from the start, it's true,
(one of the few)
They knew that I would be a wiz.
(good-bye show biz)
Life had begun and I was on the team!
(forget your dream)

So now I'm gainfully employed,
(all thanks to Dad)
Most of the time I am annoyed,
(her mood is bad)
But what I have can't be destroyed.
(she's got those)

401-K, Holiday Pay, Sick Leave, FREE Travel . . . BENEFITS!

Lack of Knowledge
Is Power

Welcome to the Corporate World

E VERY COMPANY HAS A corporate philosophy or a mission statement. This attitude usually prevails throughout the company at all levels, inwardly and outwardly. Also, most companies have some type of corporate structure. WAFTI, I discovered, is no different. As a new employee, it behooves one to learn and to understand the mission statement and the pecking order as soon as possible because it reveals so much about the company as a whole. First of all, the WAFTI mission statement: "Lower your standards, we did."

Now on to the pecking order. At WAFTI, the people at the bottom are the "peons." The peons are usually large in number, work in labor-intensive positions, and are usually the front-line employees dealing head-on with the public. Those at the next level are known as the "big shots" (secretly known as "small shots"). Usually they aren't really that important, but they're given fancy titles so they sound important. Everybody is supposed to think they're important, but most important, *they* must think they are important (kind of like the wizard in *The Wizard of Oz*). Above the big shots are the "suits." You know this group: vice presidents, CEOs, and the board. I won't discuss them at this time because at WAFTI, the peons have very little contact with suits. However, there is a close relationship between the peons and the big shots. Now there certainly are exceptions, but for the most part it seems the qualifications for becoming a big shot are as follows:

1. **Be a yes-man:** As a big shot you must possess the ability to agree with and to say "yes" to whatever a suit tells you, even if you don't agree with this directive or believe it to be right. You must nod and smile and then make it happen. This is the "puppet factor." If you do not or cannot implement these directives you will no longer be a big shot, you will either be "released from your duties" or be demoted back whence you came, to peon status. These directives most often have to do with budget cutting, productivity, and meaningless policies.

2. **Incompetence:** Basically, you should not really know what the hell you're doing. This will enable you to better get along with other big shots.

3. **The intimidation factor:** You must be able to inspire fear in all those beneath you. Threaten them, intimidate them, put the fear of God into them. Particularly when they start talking about morale, improving working conditions, and pay increases. After all, as big shots, you realize that the aforementioned have no bearing on productivity.

4. **A sense of self-importance:** You may not be qualified and capable, but so what? Lacking these qualities has no bearing on the big picture, as long as you think you are important and act as though you are important others will see you as such. Lack of knowledge is power. That's the WAFTI motto!

5. **Ability to brownnose:** This is the major qualification for a rapid rise on the corporate ladder. If you find you do not possess this asset then you can always resort to being a "tattler."*

6. **Must *not* possess any sense of humor whatsoever:** Nothing is funny, dammit! This is serious business and we don't want anyone laughing, or, for that matter, smiling. We don't have time for nonsense, fun, and games. We have a lot of paper to shuffle and things to look into and it most certainly is not funny!

---

* Whenever you see someone doing something that might not follow the WAFTI guidelines to the letter, turn them in! This will make you a hero with the suits. It will also make you feel as though you are making a valuable contribution to WAFTI and justify your paycheck.

Abandon All Hope, Ye Who Enter Here

Training

Ah, TRAINING. It is forever etched in my mind. I attribute
my successful completion of the WAFTI training program
to two things: youth and fear. The very term "trainee" is
contemptuous. You are not yet a full-fledged employee, merely a
candidate for employment. It's a purgatory, of sorts. In training, I
learned—aside from service, safety, grooming, and company policies—to keep smiling and to keep my mouth shut while being subjected to all kinds of crap. I now realize that this is basically what
flight attendants do most of the time, so perhaps there is a method
to the madness of training. There was also an element of theatrical-
ity to the program, led by the grand dame of training, June Larson.

June Larson is the big shot of the training department at
WAFTI. She is originally from a very small town somewhere
north of north, where the odds are good, but the goods are odd.
And June is living proof of it. Although she traveled around the
world back when she was a "stew" thirty years ago, she never lost
her northern accent. It is soooo cuuuute, donchya knoooow!
Have you ever heard the expression "the more you drink, the better she looks"? I think whoever came up with it was out on a ben-
der with June when it struck him. But she's been known to turn
a few heads when she enters a room—perhaps it's her platinum-
blond wig, cat glasses, and athletic physique. In any case, she
was there to give us a big, warm welcome on the first day.

"Well helloooooo everybody! I'm June Larson and I'm the head of training here at WAFTI. I just want youuuu to know I am not the enemy here, nooooo I'm not. I'm in your corner. I'm just here to help you be the best you can be." Translation: Watch it! This broad is public enemy number one. Sort of bumbling idiot on the outside with a killer instinct inside. She went on to tell us about how delighted she was to have us as part of the WAFTI family and how they were a benevolent, caring family.

"Now I want to talk about the importance of our appearance. First of all, the uniform really does begin with you, so wear it with pride." I won't make the dear reader suffer through the long speeches we endured; instead, I offer some highlights of June Larson's uniform and beauty secrets:

1. "Always use soap, deodorant, toothpaste (duh), and a light fragrance. I recommend the company-approved perfume, 'Cockpit.' Just a little airline humor, kids."
2. "Coach-class tramps don't get first-class husbands, so keep the makeup to a minimum." June did not practice what she preached. The color and amount of lipstick she wore could be seen in Montana.
3. "Earrings cannot be larger than a quarter." (Did she say earrings or *earnings*?)
4. "Hair cannot fall below the collar. And by the way, never have your top collar button unfastened, even if it is one hundred and ten degrees on the airplane and you feel like you are going to pass out from heat exhaustion. Shirts not properly buttoned look cheap and unprofessional. So what if you're hot?"
5. "Nylons, not tights, must be free from runs and worn at all times, except during an evacuation, when they should be removed because they are highly flammable and will melt onto your legs."

6. "Never leave the galley without a coffeepot in your hand and a smile on your face. A smile is the most important part of your uniform. You see, passengers have to buy their tickets, but our smiles are free. . . . You betchya!"

She then went on to explain the importance of shoes and that they had to have a certain heel size (flats are not allowed and all shoes must have between a two- and four-inch heel). "Now we want our employees to shine from head to toe, so be sure you always have your shoes shined—that means always carrying a tin of shoe polish in your tote. Our appearance checkers are stationed around the airport, and they *will* do surprise shoeshine inspections. And every few months we'll have a shoeshine contest. The winner of the contest gets a five-dollar gift certificate to the employee cafeteria, so get out there and shine!" How inspiring.

"And now I am very pleased to present the Singing Supervisors." With that she left and in came eight impeccably groomed men and women in navy suits and crisp white shirts. There was a moment of silence as they moved into a semicircle. Someone produced a black pitch pipe and someone else counted 1-2-3-4 and then the Stepford Supervisors—I mean the Singing Supervisors—broke into their rendition of the company song. I wasn't sure if should laugh or cry, but I definitely wanted to stick around because the whole scenario was morbidly fascinating. Plus the tune was kind of catchy!

The Wafti Company Song

We're sorry, we're sorry, we're sorry.
We Apologize for This Inconvenience Airlines.

Our service is bad, but it could get worse (cha-cha),
We lost your kid, but we found your purse (cha-cha),
Our food is bad, but we're not to blame,
Try another airline, it's all the same.
Sometimes we're late, but is that a crime?
Does it really matter? It's only time.

At this point a blond man with very white teeth and an orangy bottled tan dramatically broke away from the semicircle while the rest of the group continued softly singing, "Doo, doo, doo . . . cha-cha . . . doo, doo doo." He flashed his ultra-big white teeth at us and said, "Hey trainees, welcome to WAFTI! You're joining the family at a very special time because we're changing. We're upping our standards and things are getting better every day. This year ten trillion people will travel by air and that makes for some long lines at the ticket counters. So we're hiring *one* more ticket agent and *fifty* more flight attendants this year! Now we recently had to raise our fares, but we're still offering these items to our passengers at no extra charge (and you will be tested on this): free pillows, free blankets (but grab them quickly, there are only five on each plane), free overhead-bin space, and no charge for the lavatories! Yet. We've also added *two* more peanuts per bag for the hungry traveler. And although our seats are still the same small size, we've increased the length of the seat belt to give the illusion of more room.

"Things are certainly improving! But if in the rare and unlikely event that a passenger's expectations are not met, and you have done everything in your power as a service and safety professional, simply have them call the toll-free complaint hotline, 1-800-YOU'RE SCREWED . . . and one of our customer-care professionals will give them twenty free miles on WAFTI so we can have another chance to better serve them on a future trip. Twenty miles may not sound like a lot, but when people have so many complaints it really does add up quickly! Welcome aboard WAFTI, where we are upping our standards."

He then pirouetted back into the semicircle with a grace and ease that would put Tommy Tune to shame, and the entire group crescendoed into the final tag of the song with a glassy-eyed, feverous, near-religious zeal.

We Apologize for This Inconvenience Airlines
We're upping our standards (upping our standards)
Up Yours!

There was not a dry eye in the entire group of Stepford Supervisors. As for the trainees, we stood frozen in astonishment, mouths agape (almost spellbound), until someone slowly started to clap. This broke into a full round of applause as the group bowed and then went into a reprise of the tag line. More applause, and then the orange-skinned man announced that it was time for us to learn the song, and with that he went into a whirlwind frenzy of passing out sheet music that was registered, numbered, and labeled "Property of WAFTI." I guess that was meant to discourage us from stealing the sheet music. Not much chance of that.

Throughout the training program trainees were forced to endure many little indignities, not the least of which was the constant reminder that they could be released from the program at any time. One definitely sensed that big brother was watching. Even in the barracks (WAFTI housing for trainees, conveniently located on the property), we began to wonder if our dorm rooms were bugged. The instructors must have had their evaluation meetings on Thursdays because on Fridays, which were known to all trainees as Black Fridays, there would always be one or two less people in class by the end of the day. It would start out like a normal day, we would all be sitting in class, the teacher pontificating on the differences between the premeal beverage service and the postmeal beverage service when suddenly the door, always located in the back of the room, would slowly open and June Larson would appear. No one ever had the guts to actually turn around to see her, but you knew it was June because of her fragrance. She'd quietly walk up behind her victim, tap him or her on the shoulder (a move that came to be called "the claw"), then the victim and June would leave the room together. You never saw the former trainee the rest of the afternoon, or the rest of your life, for that matter. Here today, gone tomorrow. Later, one of June's underlings would come in and remove the victim's belongings and we never heard anything more about it, except for occasional sobbing or screaming as the poor sacrificial lambs made their final exit from WAFTI. It really set a great tone for the weekend, kind of livened up the atmosphere around the barracks. The survivors would spend Saturday and Sunday in paranoid states of misery, wondering why someone was dropped and who would be the next to go. Rumors would be flying around as to why the poor slob was released: "She failed too many tests!" "No, she lied on her application and they discovered she didn't really attend Harvard after all!" "Actually, what really happened is that they found out she was an ax murderer who was wanted in seven states."

These sorts of rumors would circulate all week until the next Black Friday when there would be a new victim and his or her departure became the topic of discussion throughout the following week.

Advice to New Hires

I HAVE TO ADMIT there were some close calls for me. After all, it is common for a spirited, sassy gal like myself to have sporadic altercations with authority. But somehow I escaped "the claw" and successfully completed the WAFTI training program. I was beaming with pride and relief when June Larson pinned those wings on me. The best part about graduation was learning that I had been assigned to the New York base. I was truly thrilled and eager to begin my career, which at this point I thought was going to last about six months—a precursor to my theatrical career. Well, I blinked my eyes and six months turned into sixteen years. Looking back on the first phase of my career, I wish there had been someone to take me under his or her wing and show me the ropes. As a gesture of generosity, I would like to share with any new flight attendants who might be reading this some of the knowledge I have acquired after years and years of crying—oops, I mean years and years of flying.

First of all, the real world of flying is completely unrelated to what they taught us in training. Second, seniority rules, baby! The sooner you get that into your head the better.

Being a service and safety professional is not an easy task. Most people probably aren't aware of the great choreographic skills one must possess to maneuver six beverage and meal carts around a small galley the size of a postage stamp. According to training, "the trained professional" can handle this choreography with aplomb, but the reality of it comes down to this: Do what ya gotta do to get through the meal service. For example, if you're in the left corner of the galley and need a pot of coffee from the right corner, and there are six carts between you and the coffeemaker, there is no easy way to get the coffeepot. You just have to ask your colleague, whose entire upper body is enveloped inside the meal cart while trying to find the rolls, if she would mind passing the coffeepot. First of all, she will mind because she's pissed she can't find the rolls. Second, she won't be able to hear you because she is inside a meal cart, cursing. But hey, you really do need that coffeepot, so you ask another comrade in arms, who is busy chopping up a solid block of ice that has been on a bed of dry ice for three days, if, when he has a spare moment, he could pass you the coffeepot. He looks up at you from his position on the floor for a moment, glares, and then returns to his chopping. Guess not. OK, well there is always flight attendant number three, busy pulling out 185 hot entrees from the ovens and stacking them into something that resembles a tall, tin-foiled structure and sways. This person's face is always red from the heat and she has generally developed a rhythm to her work, which does not welcome interruption. You meekly inquire what the possibility of her passing you the coffeepot might be, and she continues unloading and stacking the meals with her left hand while grabbing and passing the coffeepot to you with her right. Mission accomplished! You now have the coffeepot. Now the ice chopper needs you to pass the orange juice to him. Again, short of pole-vaulting, there is no easy way. But while a pot of scalding-hot coffee must be handled ever so gingerly, a jug of juice can be tossed across the galley like a Frisbee, and so you toss it. It goes on like this until the entire production is assembled and ready to go forth into the aisle. The meal service commences: Soup's on!

Here is where the going can get a bit rough for the new kid on the block. This is also where the seniority thing comes in. Every plane is different and every service is different, and some services are done one way if there are four flight attendants and another way if there are five. Who cares? New flight attendants care. They have to know the standard procedure on all types of planes for all types of service in all types of staffing situations. All flight attendants are supposed to follow the order of service as dictated by the manual, but as I said earlier, seniority rules on the airplane. That is, whoever is most senior on the flight runs the show and when you are brand, spanking new, everyone is senior to you. If you're smart you will quickly realize that your job is to do exactly what the senior flight attendants tell you to do. To hell with what you learned in training! However you end up slinging the hash really does not make a lot of difference as long as everyone gets fed and watered before the plane lands. On certain days, when there is a little too much estrogen in the galley, disagreements can arise among flight attendants regarding the best way to do the service. Sometimes a tiny discrepancy can erupt into a major blowout. When people ask me about air-rage incidents, what often comes to mind are arguments among flight attendants over the way to do a service, but that is another chapter entirely. So dear new hire, when the fur begins to fly it is highly advisable to *consult the manual*. Just be careful someone doesn't rip it out of your hands and throw it at you when you are reading it to them.

THE MANUAL

"F/A number 1 will deliver meals from cart number 1, working until that cart is depleted. F/As 2 and 3 will follow with beverage carts 3 and 4. When F/A number 1 has depleted cart number 1, he or she will park it at door number 2 and then go to the back galley and get cart number 2. F/As 2 and 3 will continue serving beverages.

"Meanwhile, F/A number 4 will start meals at door number 4, working forward with F/A number 5 following with beverage cart number 5. When all F/As meet in the middle, F/A number 5 will back up to the galley to allow F/As 1 and 4 to get to the back galley. Then F/A number 5 moves forward and resumes where he or she left off before making way for numbers 1 and 4. The remaining aisle flight attendants work forward until all passengers have received a beverage. Then F/A number 1 goes back to door number 2 to get the remaining empty meal cart and starts pickup service. Numbers 2 and 3 will follow with coffee, working forward while F/As 4 and 5 will do the same, working forward from door number 4. Then everybody does the hokey pokey and you turn yourself around and that's what it's all about! Note: If there are only three F/As on board follow the alternate order of service. There should never be any variation in the order of service."

By the way, this is just one service for one aircraft type, and there are at least seven types of aircraft for which flight attendants are responsible. Then there is the emergency equipment, emergency-exit operation, company policies, schedule bidding, first-aid training, handcuff operation, death on board, birth on board, CPR, how to survive a ditching (including a course titled "How to Survive at Sea"), grooming, and, most important, how the captain likes his coffee!

Everything I Need to Know About Life, I Learned in Flight Attendant Training

ASIDE FROM LEARNING about service, safety, grooming, and company policies, I learned a few other things in Flight Attendant training. Many of them have stayed with me throughout my career, and lately I've come to realize that they apply not only to my job on the airplane but also to life in general.

KNOW WHERE YOUR NEAREST EXIT IS LOCATED: Whether it is a burning airplane, a burning movie theater, or a lousy relationship. You never know when you might need to get out of something quickly.

ALWAYS HAVE A BACKUP PLAN: Life is full of surprises! The exit you picked could be blocked. Maybe that special someone you've been dating isn't your true love after all, don't wait too long . . . assess conditions and find an alternate.

EXCESS BAGGAGE: On the airplane, as in life, excess baggage is problematic. God knows most of us have it, but I have discovered that if you can't carry it, lift it, or stow it, you might as well leave it behind. Most of the time it is something that you don't need in the first place and it is just weighing you down. A lighter load makes the journey much more enjoyable.

EXPECT THE UNEXPECTED: You think you are on your way to Chicago, you are flying along when suddenly the captain makes an announcement, "Ladies and gentlemen, there is some rough weather ahead and we are low on fuel. We will have to divert and make a fuel stop in Madison." Don't panic! In all likelihood you will get to Chicago, it just might not be the way you planned. The same is true for mapping out your life; although it is good to have a destination in mind and an idea of how and when you like to arrive, you never know what rough weather, unscheduled stops, and diversions you may encounter along the way. As much as we'd like to think we are in control in making our travel plans or our life plans, we usually aren't really in control at all. Roll with the punches.

KEEP EMOTIONS AT BAY: This is a good one, especially in this day of air rage, road rage, and people rage. I can't tell you how often I have wanted to really let some passenger have it! However, if I went around swearing and screaming at people I'd be in a heap of trouble. Instead I have found it best to count to ten and make every effort to refrain from any rude, unkind comments. If a response is required, just smile and give the briefest reply and move on. Sometimes I don't say anything. I not only practice this on the airplane, but also in my everyday life. People are really shocked by silence, oftentimes the situation will be diffused right then and there. Keep cool and choose your battles wisely. Most of the time they are not worth the fight.

JUST BECAUSE IT SAYS FIRST CLASS DOESN'T MEAN IT IS: Although the term "first class" may lead one to believe that the food is better, there'll be more privacy, or the level of service will be higher, that is not always the reality. In fact, sometimes the food in coach is better, and if you can find an empty row in the back of the aircraft it is often far more comfortable than sitting by someone sprawled out next to you in that first-class seat. Also, some of the people sitting in coach class behave in a more first-class manner than some of the people actually sitting in first class. The same is true in life, being in the "first-class crowd," knowing the "heavy hitters," or hanging out with the "A-list," one might experience some of the finer things life has to offer—the gourmet food, the exquisite wine, and the ocean view—but the quality of the people in the "first-class crowd" can often belie the delicacies that may accompany this lifestyle. Sometimes you're better off with a hot dog and a true-blue friend.

ALWAYS PACK A BATHING SUIT: I have no idea what this means or why it is important. It is not as if I am going to strip off my blue polyester uniform and change into my swimsuit halfway through the flight. Nonetheless, for the last sixteen years I have been carrying around a little bikini in the bottom of my suitcase. I guess you never know when the opportunity for a little fun and frolic in a nearby pool, ocean, or lake may present itself and you wouldn't want to miss out because you neglected to pack something as simple as a swimsuit. You should always be ready to have some fun and be spontaneous . . . after all, we never know what is around the corner, it may be a beach!

The Secret Language
of Flight Attendants

HOW DOES A flight attendant say "Fuck you"?
"I'll be right back!"

Every industry has its own specific terminology. The airlines are no different. For your convenience, I've prepared a short list of terms recognized by those in the airline industry. This will help you to better understand this book, and it will also help you understand airline personnel when they say something like this: "Ladies and gentlemen, may I have your attention? The APU is INOP on the ground and ATC has put us in the HOLDING PEN, so it may be a bit uncomfortable in the cabin until we are given a slot and released. This may affect our ETA, but not our ATA because the flight time has been padded. As soon as we have a clear idea as to our ETD I will make a PA with that information."

F/A	Flight attendant
Seniority	The length of time with the company. The longer you've been around, the lower your seniority number is. The lower your seniority number is, the better for bidding.
Bidding	Choosing where you want to work on the airplane. Usually done in order of seniority.

Turnaround	A trip that leaves and returns back to base on the same day.
APU	Auxiliary Power Unit, controls air conditioning and heating.
INOP	Inoperative—broken!
ATC	Air traffic control—or God.
Holding pen	Just that, an area for overflow traffic.
ETA	Estimated time of arrival.
ATA	Actual time of arrival.
ETD	Estimated time of departure.
PA	Public announcement.
Slinging hash	Serving the meals.
On call/Reserve	Being available for a trip assignment twenty-four hours a day on select days. This is how most careers begin. As you gain seniority you'll get off reserve, and then you will have a set schedule or "line."
Screamer	A passenger who has lost his or her cool. Sort of like a "bleeder" in the medical profession.
Steerage	Coach class.
Cockpit queen	A flight attendant more interested in the front

end of the aircraft than in the chamber of horrors known as the "cabin."

Crop dusting	Walking down the aisle while inconspicuously passing gas.
UM	Unaccompanied minor. A child traveling alone, usually sweet and and charming. Can sometimes be challenging. Definitely challenging when there are ten or more on board, which is often the case during summer or Christmas break.
Debriefing	Party in someone's room after a flight.
Pax	Slang for passengers.
Upgrade	A passenger who has moved up from economy or business class to first class. Upgrades are recognizable by the way they demand refills on their cocktails every five minutes because they are free.
Load	Refers to the number of passengers on board, as in, "What is the load today?" When it comes to loads, my favorite phrase is, "We have light loads all day today!"
Widebody	This usually refers to the 747 aircraft, which is also known as "the Whale." Often we will use this term to describe a person, as in "Check out the outfit that widebody is wearing!"
3-holer	This is an aircraft with three engines, such as a 727. For sixteen years I was under the

impression that it meant three pilots. Like three assholes in the cockpit. Not that I think pilots are assholes. They are not (most of them anyway).

Blue room	This is what is known as the lav, the biffy, the john, or the bathroom.
Jumpseat	And you thought your seat was uncomfortable! This is the seat that flight attendants occupy for takeoff and landing. It's to be used by crew members only, and it is not a footrest for those passengers seated across from it. Thank you.
Tuff cuff	Plastic handcuffs for those unruly disruptive passengers. "Disruptive" includes, but is not limited to, carving initials on the window with a penknife, unwanted sexual remarks or advances (this may include the captain), and running down the aisle naked (yes, it has happened, and if you can catch the perpetrator the tuff cuffs do come in handy).
Over the pond	Flying over the Atlantic or Pacific, as in, "It's going to be a little rough going over the pond today."
Slam click	On a layover, when a flight attendant goes directly to his or her room instead of going out with the crew. "I was so tired last night, I slam clicked." Derived from the sound of the hotel door being shut and locked.
Crash pad	Housing near the airport where about a million flight attendants (most often new hires or commuters) shack up together. Basically it's a cheap

	place to sleep in the event you have an earlier departure or two trips back to back. You never know who you might find yourself in bed with. The other alternative is sleeping at the airport.
Pilot blocks	A block that's three miles long. You'll make plans for dinner on your layover and the captain will suggest a restaurant and say that it's only about a two-block walk, which translates to a six-mile walk.
Just a few moments	A long time. A very long time.
Equipment change	Broken aircraft.

Do You Have a Place to Stow My Cheesecake?

I REALLY WANT TO EMPHASIZE the amount of psychological stress associated with being a flight attendant, especially a new hire. You don't know the ropes yet, and you've probably just moved to a new city and live in some scummy apartment with four or five other stressed-out novice flight attendants. You're on reserve and never know where the hell you're going or when you'll be back. Once you arrive at work you'll be subjected to all sorts of bullshit. It starts the minute you walk in the door: Some big shot will be giving you the once-over. Is your hair right? Are you wearing your uniform properly? Frankly, I think it's a big accomplishment if I can *find* my uniform. The supervisor may call you into the office and ask you about some outraged passenger on a flight three months ago, but you won't be able to recall this incident because there have been hundreds of flights since then and they've all been full of outraged passengers!

Then it is time to meet the crew. If you're lucky you'll be with a nice, fun, cooperative group of people. This is usually the case, but every now and again you end up with some real oddballs and, believe me, these freaks can make a simple two-day trip a living hell. Now it is time to board the plane. This is where things will most likely be screwed up. For example, there is usually a shortage of supplies—like food! Once you make this discovery, tell someone right away. If you delay because you want enough food so all the passengers can eat, you will be getting a call on your layover and someone is going to want to know why the flight left three seconds late. Never mind that you were missing twenty meals! I once heard of a crew that was so short on breakfasts (boxed cereal, wrapped bagel, and apples) that they didn't have enough food to get past row twenty-two. So they fed the front half of the plane, then went through and collected the uneaten and unopened leftovers from the first twenty-two rows and then offered these leftovers to those passengers in rows twenty-two to twenty-eight. For psychological stress some people recommend therapy, but I recommend *denial*. It's a lot cheaper and easier to schedule. I spent years of my career in denial and look at me, I lived to tell the tale!

The next piece of advice I offer to the new hire is to develop the virtue of *patience*. If you don't have this you are doomed! Forget about carrying a tin of shoe polish in your tote, you better have the patience of Job in your pocket, because it is going to be tested . . . daily. Let me start by saying that you're going to say "hello," "good-bye," and "I'm sorry" to a hell of a lot of people in the course of a day, let alone the course of a career. You'll be giving the safety demonstration sometimes five times a day (sometimes more), offering coffee hundreds of times a day, and in this global economy in which we are now living, you will be conversing or at least attempting to converse with people from all over the world. One of the greatest joys of this profession is all the intellectual stimulation it provides. Oh yes indeed, flight attendants are permitted to engage in so many enervating conversations with passengers. They usually begin with one of the following questions:

Will our luggage make it?
Can you get me a pillow?

Will I make my connection?
Do you have raspberry kiwi iced tea?
Is this decaf?
Is that your natural hair color?
Has anyone ever told you that you resemble Monica
    Lewinsky?
What time is it?
Is this your regular route?
Can I borrow your pen?
Can you find out the score of the game?
Why?
Why not?
Where?
When?
Who?
What river is that?
Where are we?
Can I have another bag of peanuts?
Can I have the whole can?
Doesn't the air-conditioning work on this airplane?
Is this your regular route?
Where do you live?
Are you married?
Have you ever been married?
Do you have a boyfriend?
Have you ever had a boyfriend?
How old are you?
Can I have another beer?
Where is my seat?
Can you bring me drinking water?
Where can I hang my wedding dress?
So, you live in New York. . . . Why?

What's your rent?
Can I use your Chapstick?
Who is in charge here?
Why can't I use my cell phone?
Can I move up to first class?
Do you have a refrigerator?
Is this your regular route?
Do you have soy milk?
Who is flying the plane?
Can you heat this up in the microwave for me?
Where are you staying tonight?
Is this your regular route?
Can you take this diaper?
Do you have a place I can stow my cheesecake?

As I mentioned, many times these questions *can* lead to in-depth conversations regarding important issues like world peace, global warming, and the economics of underdeveloped nations. They also lead to discussions about major life decisions, such as what type of light snack a passenger might enjoy on a particular day.

FLIGHT ATTENDANT: Hello. Would you like the almond rocca or the brownie?

PASSENGER (very long pause with a blank stare): What?

FLIGHT ATTENDANT: Would you like the almond rocca or the brownie today?

PASSENGER: What?

FLIGHT ATTENDANT: Would you like the almond rocca or the brownie today?

PASSENGER: What did you say?

FLIGHT ATTENDANT: Would . . . you . . . like . . . the . . . almond . . . rocca . . . or . . . the . . . brownie . . . TODAY?

PASSENGER: Ohhhhh. . . . Well, ummm, brownie . . . I guess. . . .

FLIGHT ATTENDANT: OK, here you go. . . . Jesus Christ! (The "Jesus Christ" is whispered under the breath, of course.)

FLIGHT ATTENDANT: Hello, would you like the almond rocca or the brownie, sir?

NEXT PASSENGER: What?

FLIGHT ATTENDANT: Would you like the almond rocca or the brownie?

PASSENGER: Ummmm, what?

FLIGHT ATTENDANT: You know, you could probably hear me a lot better if you took those headphones off. OK, now, would you like the almond rocca or the brownie?

PASSENGER: Do you have any peanuts?

FLIGHT ATTENDANT: No.

PASSENGER: Can I get a Coke?

FLIGHT ATTENDANT: Yes, it's on the beverage cart behind me, sir.

PASSENGER: What is that?

FLIGHT ATTENDANT: It's a cart with drinks on it.

PASSENGER: No, that pink thing in your hand. What is that?

FLIGHT ATTENDANT: That is the almond rocca.

PASSENGER: I thought you said you had brownies.

FLIGHT ATTENDANT: Look pal . . .

PASSENGER: Well, what is almond rocca anyway?

FLIGHT ATTENDANT: It is a fine butter toffee elegantly wrapped in gold foil. Now do you want one or not?

PASSENGER (pouting): Nah, nothing.

FLIGHT ATTENDANT: Fine. Buh-bye.

FLIGHT ATTENDANT: Hello, would you like the almond rocca or the brownie?

PASSENGER: Listen, my husband and I were separated . . .

FLIGHT ATTENDANT: Yeah, well, nothing lasts forever.

PASSENGER: No, I mean we were not seated together. We purchased these tickets six months ago and we were promised two seats together, and I'd like you to do something about it.

FLIGHT ATTENDANT: There is not much I can do about it now, but after I deliver all the almond roccas and brownies, I can try to see if someone will switch seats with you.

PASSENGER: You are going to do something about it right now, young lady. Do you know who I am? DO YOU KNOW WHO I AM? Well, do you?

FLIGHT ATTENDANT (over public address system): Ladies and gentlemen, may I have your attention please? We have a passenger on board who does not seem to know who she is. If anyone can identify her, please ring your flight attendant call button.

FLIGHT ATTENDANT (to next passenger): Would you like the almond rocca or the brownie?

PASSENGER: I'll have the almond brownie!

FLIGHT ATTENDANT: I'll be right back.

Seeking SWF F/A
to Share Manhattan Apt
$400 Per Month or Less

AFTER TRAINING, being assigned to the New York base seemed like a dream come true. I was convinced that I'd be able to have my cake and eat it too—that is, I would have this airline job with *benefits* and also be able to pursue my acting career in the Big Apple. Little did I know what lay ahead. First of all, I had nowhere to live, let alone any kind of theatrical connections. Youth gave me a kind of indefatigable confidence that I could do anything and that something would work out. Of course it did, but it wasn't exactly what I had planned.

I pictured myself living in a swanky Manhattan apartment. It might be small to start out, but eventually (like within a month or two) I'd have some great digs. Just before graduation WAFTI sent us out on a one-day base-familiarization trip. The minute we arrived in New York I began scouring the board with advertisements for available apartments, sublets, and that sort of thing. My aim was to find another female flight attendant who had her own apartment in Manhattan and was willing to share it for less than $400 a month. What can you say about a young chick from the Midwest, except that ignorance is bliss? Needless to say, there was no such situation available. In fact, much to my chagrin, there was not even one notice on the board regarding housing. The only notices appearing before me were a "never worn wedding dress for sale . . . cheap" and a 1979 SAAB in excellent condition that was also up for grabs. Would it be possible to live in a SAAB?

It was then that I met Olive Douglas, a seasoned, sassy New York flight attendant. She listened to my tale of woe and said, with the cadence of a native New Yorker, "donworryaboutit." It turned out that Olive knew of some flight attendants who were looking for a new housemate. "Whaddya know?" They worked for a charter company, and had a big house in Queens near the airport. These men were great—all five of them—and I'd have my own room, all for $300 a month. And there was no lease. I had to find something and I figured if it didn't work out, I could get out of it easily enough and the price was certainly right. (I was about to discover the meaning of the phrase "you get what you pay for.")

"So whaddya say?"

"Ummm, is there any way I could see the place or at least talk to the people who live there before I make a decision?"

"Look, I'm givin' youse a great opportunity here. I make all the arrangements and anyway the boys are all out of town this week. The place is great, ya gotta just trust me. Besides, what other options do ya have?" As she asked me this, she eyeballed the "never worn" wedding dress sign.

I had to think fast. I didn't really like the idea of living with complete and utter strangers—five men, no less! Queens was not exactly Manhattan, but these people did not work for WAFTI. Maybe that was a good thing. Ahh, what to do? I looked around at the desperate, frightened faces of my classmates, who were also trying to find places to live. Olive was working a buyers' market. If I said no someone else would jump on this and then where would I be? Living in the SAAB.

"Okay Olive, I'll take it. I'll be out here next week. Can I move in then?"

"Sure, donworryaboutit, no problem."

Olive and I worked out the details regarding keys and phone numbers and then she gave me the address. My first New York address: 22 Lefferts Blvd., Top Floor. It wasn't exactly Fifth Avenue. In fact, it was about as far away from Fifth Avenue as a girl could get, and yet I was thrilled. I had found a place in New York on my own and I was now about to embark on a journey that held all sorts of possibilities.

I began making my plans. As soon as I was settled, I would start my acting classes, get new head shots, find an agent, and start looking for an apartment in Manhattan. Oh yeah . . . and fly a few trips. After all, my first priority would have to be my job. I arranged to have my boxes shipped out (courtesy of WAFTI). I had a lot of boxes because I planned on staying in New York, and since the shipping was free I decided to take advantage and get as many of my personal effects as possible (like my clothes, books, cross-country skis, tennis racket, roller skates, and assorted other necessities, not least of which included my stereo, the speakers, and about three hundred albums—this was the eighties) sent to my new home, 22 Lefferts Blvd., Top Floor. I had arrived! I had a roof over my head and a song in my heart.

Il Fait Souffrir
(One Must Suffer)

ALL TOO SOON I discovered the song in my heart was the blues. This living-in-Queens thing was worse than I imagined. To put it mildly, it sucked. My housemates were colorful (to say the least), and the ringleader had a flair for drama and a hot temper the likes of which I'd never seen. Combine the temper with a few vodkas and you had quite a lethal combination. He was home a lot and unhappy. I was home a lot, too, so we spent a great deal of time together. Joy. Why was I home so much? After all, this was my new life, wasn't I the one who was going to take acting classes, get an agent, and be a star? Yeah, that was the plan, but in making these plans I forgot to include the part about being on reserve with WAFTI. You know, sitting on call twenty days out of the month, ready to be at the airport with one hour's notice (and no beeper allowed)! Sometimes I would fly ten days in a row. I felt as though I lived in my uniform and the only good thing I can say about that is that it reduces your dry-cleaning bill considerably. If you never take it off, you can't get it dry-cleaned!

Plus, getting in and out of Manhattan was no small feat. I had to walk eight blocks and then take two trains. I could really go in only on my days off, which were irregular, thus making it difficult to take classes consistently or to attend auditions. It also made it difficult to look for an apartment. You see, I discovered that in

New York there is a whole system to obtaining a decent, or for that matter an indecent, apartment. To begin with, you have to decide whether you wish to navigate the stormy sea of rental properties alone or with the assistance of a broker. Going it alone requires a lot of phone-calling, running around, and encountering some unsavory characters along the way. Enlisting the services of a broker also requires a lot of phone-calling, running around, encountering unsavory characters, and shelling out a *huge* sum of cash to the broker in the event he or she finds something for you. The advantage to using a broker is that if you're fortunate enough to hook up with a good one, he or she can speed the process along and prevent you from going on some wild-goose chases. I didn't have the money to use a broker or the time to go on a wild-goose chase, so I simply stayed where I was—22 Lefferts Blvd., Top Floor. It was sort of like a bad marriage.

Actually, the housing thing was the least of my problems. The guys were nice and for the most part they were gone for eight- or nine-day stretches. Even the ringleader had to fly his trips, so often I was alone in Queens, just waiting for a trip. Sometimes it would be two or three days of waiting, and I cried a lot. I began to feel that I had made a horrible mistake with my life. I wanted to go home, and yet I didn't want to just give up. I had come this far and I was finally in the Big Apple. Eventually, I would get off reserve and hold a set schedule. In the meantime I would just have to endure my miserable, wretched life. And let me tell you, it was miserable. I'm the type of person who likes to sleep at night and be awake during the day. However, when you're flying on reserve you might be working a red-eye one night and then working a trip that has a 5:00 A.M. check-in one day later. Your time clock is completely shot. I also like to have a modicum of control over my existence. Who doesn't? Being on reserve, you might as well throw the idea of control out the window. You're controlled by central scheduling, so you're no longer a human being with needs such as sleep, food, and regularity. No, you're merely a number, a body required to fulfill the minimum number of crew members on board an air-craft bound for somewhere (and often nowhere). Not only that, when you finally do get let out of your cage and assigned a trip, you're at the bottom of the barrel when you bid in with the crew. This translates to having absolutely no choice of where you work on the airplane. Bidding for your working position is done in order of seniority from the most senior flight attendant down to the most junior flight attendant. Junior flight attendants get what nobody else wants, and, believe me, there is a reason nobody else wants those positions. Eventually one works one's way up the seniority list, but it takes an eternity! So there I was, living in Queens, at the bottom of the seniority list, trying to grow out my bad training hair-cut and battling constant jet lag. I pretty much looked like crap most of the time. I realized that I had never known the true mean-ing of the word "exhaustion" until I became an international air hostess. Even to this day I wonder what long-term effect crossing the international date line so often has had on me. I remember one hellish week in July: I was lying in the sun (supposedly this allevi-ates jet lag) on the tar roof outside my bedroom window, fondly known as "Tar Beach." I had the tunes cranked and the phone stretched out from the hall onto the ledge. It wasn't exactly Saint-Tropez, but it was better than sitting in the house watching *General Hospital. Riiiinnng!* The phone rang, ripping me from a sweaty slumber. It was scheduling.

"We have a London trip for you leaving at nine P.M. tonight, short London layover, returning on the third day. Check in at JFK at seven-thirty P.M. Thank you." *Click.*

Most people would be excited about the prospect of going to London, albeit for less than twenty-four hours, but not me. I was getting sick of London. I was still tired from my trip the day before, and definitely not in the mood to force myself to stay awake all night serving a full ship of Brits, only to arrive just as the sun is rising in jolly old England. But what choice did I have? I, of course, flew the trip and made it back to JFK three days later. The worst part came when I arrived back home at 22 Lefferts Blvd., Top Floor. It was about 2:00 P.M. when I walked into the house, stripping off my nylons and polyester uniform, to the dreaded ringing of the phone.

"Hello?"

"This is scheduling for flight attendant Foss, we have a trip for you."

"What? I just got in from London. I can't possibly go anywhere else today."

"The trip is for tomorrow. Tokyo, departing at three-thirty P.M., check-in is at one P.M. Thank you." *Click.*

"Ahhhhhhh, my God, my God, why hast thou forsaken me like this?!" I screamed. Coming in from London one day and then going off to Tokyo (which is geographically on the other side of the world) the very next day cannot be conducive to good mental or physical health. Not to mention the trip is fourteen hours in the air, if everything goes accordingly. Sometimes there is a fuel stop in Anchorage, making it even longer. I wanted to scream and claw my face. Fortunately, I resisted the urge and took a cold shower instead. Yes, I flew the trip, and I think it was at that point that I came up with the phrase "Around the world in a bad mood."

Looking back, I guess the only good thing was that I met Bitsy Heatherton on that trip. Who in the hell is Bitsy Heatherton, you may be asking yourself? She is another flight attendant, and she had recently transferred to the New York base. She was looking for a roommate to share a studio apartment with her in Manhattan. Maybe things were turning around. God knows, they couldn't get any worse.

Manhattan
Capital of Reality

T HANKS TO BITSY HEATHERTON I was able to finally make the long-awaited move from Queens to Manhattan. She was desperately looking for a roommate to replace her last one, who could no longer handle the glamorous excitement of the airline industry. While on an Athens layover her roommate had called the company and said, "I quit!" She had a Greek lover who apparently offered her a brighter future than did a career as an international airline hostess. Anyway, she was gone and Bitsy needed someone right away. It was my golden opportunity to move to Manhattan.

Getting there was not easy, figuratively or literally. I did not have a car, but I did have a lot of stuff, some of which I never even got around to unpacking. My dilemma: how to get all my boxes, stereo, cross-country skis, and the little furniture I had acquired in Queens into Manhattan. I began by putting a few of my boxes on my luggage cart and some of my clothes into a garment bag, which rested on top of the cart. From there I proceeded out the front door, dragging the entire ensemble behind me to the local subway station, where I caught the F train into Manhattan. Then I took a bus up to the new place. After about three round-trips I was exhausted, and it seemed that I had not made much of a dent in getting things moved out of there. Also, there were a number of things I needed to move that could not be taken on public transportation. I began throwing things away, and finally decided to move the rest of it in a cab. Fortunately for me I met up with a delightful cab driver. His name was Victor and he fell in love with me as he helped me load the Panasonic stereo into the trunk of his gypsy cab. Now, I'm not sure if Victor had car insurance, or even a license for that matter, but without his help I don't think I would have been able to get everything to my new home. His English was limited, but we were able to communicate enough for him to ask if he could take Bitsy and me out for dinner. We accepted. And so the first official night at my new home in Manhattan was spent having pizza and a cheap bottle of Chianti at a dive on Second Avenue with my new room-mate and my new friend, Victor the Albanian gypsy-cab driver.

It may not have been a palace, but Bitsy and I loved living in our little studio on the Upper East Side. The rent was $750 a month, which isn't a lot—especially when you divide it by two—but we weren't making the big bucks yet. And we were living in Manhattan, so every time we walked out the door we spent $20 on something. We decided to take a few more girls in on a temporary basis in order to reduce the rent. We weren't concerned about crowding because we would all be on different schedules. It was unlikely that we would all be there at the same time, so we bought a futon and plastic shelf unit and Bitsy and I decided to share the closet. We didn't have any intention of hanging around the apart- ment that much anyway; I was going to be a big star and she was out to meet a rich man and be a socialite. Now that we were no longer on reserve and were holding schedules (crappy ones, but schedules nonetheless), we were ready to set the world on fire!

I was flying trips to Madrid, and although I love Madrid and enjoyed being there once I arrived, *getting there* required an enor- mous amount of intestinal fortitude. I never knew just how diffi- cult it could be to drag my ass from point A to point B until I became a flight attendant. To begin with, Bitsy and I lived on the fifth floor of a five-story walk-up, so every time I came home from a trip I had to navigate the stairs with my luggage cart. At this point in history the ever popular rollerboard had not yet come into fashion, so I had two blue WAFTI-issued bags that had to be arranged on separate carts and then tied together with a bungee cord. Leaving the apartment, once I made it down the stairs, in my blue polyester uniform including my blue pumps with two-inch heels, I had to schlep six blocks to the Lexington Avenue subway and then trudge down another flight of stairs against a teeming assemblage of other harried New Yorkers coming up the same stairway. The next obstacle was maneuvering my way through the turnstile. And then there's the lengthy wait on the platform (this part was particularly horrid in the summer months because of the sweltering heat, which was only made worse by the oppressive polyester uniform). And then finally boarding, and usually standing on a jampacked number 6 train downtown to Grand Central Station, where I would catch the Carey bus to JFK Airport.

I'd only allow myself the luxury of a taxi if Bitsy or one of the other assorted roommates was also going on a trip to Grand Central at the same time. Taxis were a nonessential item that did not fit into my tight budget. I could hardly afford to take a taxi from the apartment to the Carey bus, so taking a taxi all the way to the airport was completely out of the question, although I longed to do it quite often. In any case, getting to the Carey bus was just the first leg of what was a long day's journey into night. Once I arrived at JFK I had to hustle up to the check-in office where I checked in, met my crew, and got our flight information. We then boarded the limo (really a big van that smells of stale car freshener combined with patchouli oil) bound for LaGuardia Airport, where our trip would begin. Why didn't we just check in at LaGuardia and eliminate the hassle of going out to JFK? Because that would make sense. One of the phenomenons I've discovered about the airline industry is that the less something makes sense, the more likely it is to become a standard operating procedure. So, along with seven other flight attendants, I would settle into the limo for a nice long ride in rush-hour traffic from JFK to LaGuardia.

Upon our arrival we would then hurry over, en masse, to the 5:00 P.M. shuttle and fly, as passengers, up to Boston, where we would have a two-hour sit before our 9:00 P.M. flight to Madrid. Since I left my apartment at 1:00 P.M. I had already put in an eight-hour day, but according to WAFTI the workday was just beginning. Alas, the time clock does not start until the captain starts the engine. At that point we still had an eight-hour flight ahead of us—providing there were no delays—and then another hour to get to the hotel and sign in for our rooms. Often the rooms would not be ready for new occupants and so the available rooms were given out in seniority order. In other words, the junior people on the crew would have to wait in the lobby. I've fallen asleep in the lobby of many a hotel in this world while waiting for my cell—uh, I mean, room.

The worst part of this was that it was my weekly schedule; I had to do five of these three-day trips a month. After about three months I was getting burned out and pretty ragged around the edges. I was already a haggard battle-ax of a gal at the ripe old age of twenty-four. However, I was not as bad as some—at least not yet. I'll admit it, I have met some flight attendants who have scared the hell out of me. I'm sure you know the type because they terrorize everyone on the plane: "Fasten that seat belt!" they bark as they come up the aisle, slamming the seat backs of poor slobs who haven't returned to the upright, locked position as previously ordered. In short, these flight attendants possess all the charm and conviviality of the Newark Airport parking lot at about 4:00 A.M.

Mona Lott

"TESTING, ONE-TWO-THREE. ... hello? Is this thing on? Oh, for Christ's sake. ... OK. Welcome aboard We Apologize for This Inconvenience Airlines, also known as WAFTI. OK, this is flight 5050 to, ummm . . . to . . . let's see here, today we are going to . . . umm, well we will figure that out later, ummm, it's on your ticket if you really need to know. This flight is under the command of Captain Booze, assisted by First Officer Chance, and as we like to say here at WAFTI, if Booze and Chance can't get ya there . . . nothing can! All right then, moving on. My name is Mona—Mona Lott—and I'm your senior indentured servant for this flight. Once airborne, if we should ever live to see the day, this flight will take about four hours to get to wherever the hell we're going! We will not be showing a movie on today's flight because we don't feel like passing out the headsets, plus people never have the correct change and I'm getting sick of spending the whole flight trying to change a fifty when I could be sitting in my jumpseat reading *People* magazine. Now for your comfort we have four lavatories on this aircraft: one in first class and three in coach. However, only one is working, so pace yourself on the drinks! The airphones are not working, we have only three pillows and two blankets, and we're short two flight attendants, fifty-five meals, and one good engine. And by the way, this flight is oversold. We do not have any magazines or newspapers, but we do have the pamphlet *How to Deal with Anger in a Positive Non-violent Way*. Today we will be passing these pamphlets out in lieu of the meals. In the meantime, please remember that to be human is to know pain and suffering and to be a prisoner—I mean, a passenger—on WAFTI is to know rage. We here at WAFTI appreciate your business and we want you to know that we're constantly upping our standards. . . . So up yours!

"Now it is time for the safety demonstration. This information could save your life so please pay attention, and remember ladies and gentlemen, next time your plans include air travel, wherever your final destination may be, please keep this thought in mind: Flight attendants are on board the aircraft to save your ass, not kiss it! Is my crew ready? All right, it's time for the 'Safety Demo Shuffle.' I will now be dimming the cabin lights to enhance the beauty of our flight attendants. Oh yes, one more thing: When the captain turns on the seat-belt sign I want to hear *one* click! Sit back, relax, and enjoy your trip."

SAFETY DEMO SHUFFLE

If you've never traveled by car
this is your seat belt, please know
where they are. To fasten the belt,
just pull till it's tight and don't let
go till the end of the flight!
This is for safety, especially yours, pay
close attention as we point out the doors,
please keep in mind this aircraft has eight,
they all have slides and we hope they inflate.
If we have to get out, there won't be much time,

so head for the door and follow in line, should the
cabin lose pressure, place this mask on your nose,
if the plane's going down, just reach for your toes,
  if we have a water evacuation, use your tushy
  cushion for your flotation, pull up and remove,
  then hold to your chest, dive in the water, and
                      hope for the best!
   A few more reminders, then off on our way:
   No smoking, no cell phones, no meals today!
   Thank you for flying, we're glad to arrive.
    If you want to get there faster, if you want
  to get there sooner, if you just want to get there
      why don't you drive??? We dooooooo!!!!!

Melrose Place?

So, there I was living in a studio apartment with Bitsy and a bunch of other new flight attendants who came as quickly as they left. To call it an ever-changing cast of characters would be an understatement. We did have a lot of fun, and the neighbors thought it was something to have all these wacky chicks coming and going. And wacky we were!

I had started taking voice lessons and could be heard vocalizing at odd times of the day. I was also taking tap-dance lessons, and when none of the other girls was around I would practice my tap and vocalize at the same time, killing two birds with one stone. We also had a girl from Alabama living with us for the summer, Kitty O'Malley. Although she was a bit older, she was junior to us because she had started three months after we did. Kitty was quite pretty, recently divorced, and glad to be out of Alabama. She had a Southern drawl and a general Southern charm that drove the men crazy. Often I would come home from a trip to find Kitty sitting on the futon, sipping champagne with some Wall Street guy who was hoping to get to know Kitty a bit better. I always hated to break up the party, but I was exhausted and there was a house rule that those coming in or going out on a trip called the shots. Since I had just come in from a trip, whatever I said was the law of the land. After all, it was a one-room apartment. In any case, I think my wanting to lie in bed and watch television might have taken something away from their romantic evening. Kitty never seemed to mind, but I certainly got some evil looks from her assorted dates. Actually, the general layout of the place didn't really inspire romance. You walked in the front door and there you were in the middle of the kitchen. To the right was a little dressing area and a small bathroom, which always had panty hose, slips, and other hand washables hanging in the shower. To the left was a perfectly square room that had two tall windows that looked out to a brick wall. We had furnished it with two single beds (in front of each window), a futon across from one bed, and a tall plastic collapsing shelf unit across from the other. We also had some folding lawn chairs that we stored behind the shelf unit. There were always suitcases and uniform pieces strewn about the place, which gave it the feel of a flophouse rather than the pied-à-terre of international flight attendants. Bitsy had filled her side of the shelf unit with her mug collection. She had recently entered a phase where she was questioning her career: "What is the point of this insipid little job anyway?" she asked us daily. "All I have to show for the last four years of my life is a mug collection. Some people have homes, cars, kids, husbands. I have mugs." Her mug collection consisted of a mug from every city she had ever visited, even if it was just to get off the airplane to buy a mug. Some of the mugs were pretty ugly, but they meant the world to her so we never asked her to get rid of them. They kind of grew on us after awhile.

Bitsy, Kitty, and I also had another girl living with us on a part-time basis. Her name was Rose. She had been flying for ten years and held terrific trips to Asia. She really lived in Phoenix, but since there was no base there Rose had to fly into New York the day before her trip. She always needed a place to spend the night. This is what's known as "commuting." Some people think it's a big deal to have to commute an hour to work by car. People in the airline industry often spend eight hours getting to work by plane, and that's pretty much what Rose did. She would leave

Phoenix on the first flight bound for JFK; if she didn't get on that one she would have to wait around for the next one. When and if she got to JFK she would then have to take the Carey bus into the city, and then a subway or cab up to the apartment. Then the next morning she'd have to get up and get ready and go back out to JFK for the trip she was assigned to work, and when she finished the trip three or four days later she would just hop on a flight back to Phoenix. If for any reason she missed the flight or couldn't get one, she would come and stay at the apartment again. Why would someone put themselves through this torture—and believe it or not a great many airline pilots and flight attendants do—just to get to work? Because they want to live where they want to live, and if there's not a base in that city then they have to get to a city where there is a base. Since we airline employees can fly for free, why not? It's complicated, but definitely part of the airline life.

Anyway, one hot August night all four of us went out carousing around the Upper East Side: smoking, drinking, and looking for men. Unsuccessful, we went home to the apartment, which lacked air-conditioning. We were all drunk as hoot owls. We were also a bit irritable because it was crowded with all four of us there at the same time and it was so bloody hot—even with the windows wide open and two fans blowing it still felt like an oven. None of us could fall asleep. Bitsy and I were each in our respective beds, and Kitty and Rose shared the futon.

"We should close the windows, it just brings more hot air in here," Bitsy pointed out.

"I don't think so, if we close the windows we will just trap the heat inside; at least this way if there is a bit of a breeze, we might feel it," Rose argued. We discussed this subject for about fifteen minutes and then Kitty got up, stumbled to the bathroom, and began taking a shower. She returned to her futon naked, with a bath towel soaked in cold water, and laid the cold, wet towel on top of her. I thought this was odd, but she said it felt wonderful and began to doze off. Then Rose decided to try this remedy, and it seemed to work just as well for her. I was next, and Bitsy was last. By the time Bitsy returned from the shower the rest of us had fallen asleep. Somehow in the darkness—with all the naked bodies and luggage lying about the place—Bitsy accidentally tripped. She tried to save herself from falling to the ground by grabbing the collapsible shelf unit. Unfortunately for Bitsy, the collapsible shelf unit collapsed, and all her mugs fell to the ground with a great crash. "Goddamnit, there go my mugs," she screamed. "All I have to show for my miserable, banal, rotten life lies before me, shattered in a million pieces!"

We spent the next day taking inventory of which mugs had survived the great crash and which would have to be replaced. Billings, Paris, Chicago, Rio de Janeiro, Baton Rouge, Dallas, Cozumel, Aspen, and San Diego all survived. We were sad, however, to report that Boston; Washington, D.C.; Dublin; Tokyo; Lisbon; and Nashville were permanently destroyed. It would be very difficult to replace some of the goners because we had discontinued service to some of those cities. This was very disheartening for Bitsy because she figured that the ruined mugs represented at least two years of her life—gone in one fleeting moment. We observed a moment of silence in honor and in memory of the forever-lost mugs.

Although we all felt sad for Bitsy, the loss seemed to give her a renewed interest in her flying career. She decided to replace each and every one of those lost mugs and even to add new mugs to the collection. "The phrase 'meaningful employment' has significance for me now. This has helped me find purpose in my job, my raison d'être. Finally, I have a career goal! I think I am going to pull through," she said as she wiped away her tears and applied a fresh coat of lipstick.

Unleashed Gluttony

I T I S N O W O N D E R we have an obesity epidemic in this country. Instead of trying to assuage the hunger of their souls with something meaningful and significant, people seem to choose to satisfy it with extra-large Diet Cokes, sugary doughnuts, greasy hamburgers, potato chips, and anything else that gives instant gratification and temporary fulfillment. Nowhere is this more apparent than on an airplane where you a have a cross section of society.

FLIGHT ATTENDANT: Hello, can I get you a beverage?
PASSENGER: Yes, I'll have a can of tomato juice, a bottle of water, and two cups of coffee with cream and sugar.
FLIGHT ATTENDANT: Are you ordering for the whole row?
PASSENGER: No, that's just for me. . . . I'm kind of thirsty.
FLIGHT ATTENDANT: I guess. Anything else?
PASSENGER: Yeah, now that you mention it, I'll have a can of apple juice for later.

In addition to the rampant gluttony, I have also noticed that a great many people are completely unaware of anyone or anything else around them. I guess it's what you might call complete and total self-absorption. Recently, a passenger went in between two beverage carts while trying to get to his seat. Instead of recognizing that he was causing the flight attendants a lot of difficulty in serving the other passengers, he just stood there with his head-phones on, doing some kind of Tai Chi stretches in the aisle.

Early in my career I witnessed a wonderful payback that illustrates the overall consciousness of certain people on the planet these days. A flight attendant was walking down the nar-row aisle of the aircraft and she was carrying a stack of about six dirty dinner trays—one on top of the other—back to the galley. A very large passenger was walking up the aisle, and as he tried to navigate around the flight attendant he said, "Hey, get me a Coke, will ya? I'm thirsty." Without missing a beat, the flight attendant answered, "Oh, you need a Coke, do you? Well here, hold these and I'll be glad to get you one." With that she handed him the dirty trays and then very slowly walked back to the galley and poured him his drink.

Airline food has been the butt of many jokes over the years. People make fun of its quality, color, taste (or lack thereof), but as soon as you take it away people miss it! People used to complain about the food choices we offered: "All you have are three choices?! And all of them terrible! My God, what is the world coming to?" Then as we incurred some cutbacks and started giving everyone the same meal, people were downright appalled: "You mean every-one is getting the chicken? This is horrifying, I can't believe I don't have a goddamn choice!" To that fine gentleman I replied, "But sir, you do have a choice: eat or don't." Now, as cost-cutting measures continue, we have not only eliminated the choice, but on certain flights we've eliminated the meal service altogether.

Just the other day a passenger reamed me out about the fact that there was no meal service on a one-hour flight at two in the afternoon. "What kind of cheap-ass airline is this anyway?" he inquired.

"One of the finest," I said. He didn't appreciate my humor (they never do), and so I will now take this opportunity to address the food situation and hopefully put an end to all the malarkey about airline cuisine. *Airlines are in the transportation business, not the restaurant business!* The primary reason they put food on airplanes in the first place was to occupy the passengers during long flights when commercial air travel was new to the world. They should have put in libraries instead, but no, somebody had to come up with the idea of serving six-course meals. There have been many noble attempts over the years to create the impression of a five-star dining experience at thirty-nine thousand feet: regional variations, world-renowned chefs, elegant china, and the dreaded "special" meal. But these days it's more about logistics, portion control, and profit margin than fine dining—and everybody is pissed! Simply put, fine "whining" has replaced fine dining. When the airline tells you they'll be serving a five-course meal, it means an apple, a granola bar, cheese, crackers, and a mint in a paper bag.

The best way to handle this unfortunate reality is to lower your expectations. You might even try the self-reliance thing— you know, carrying a small supply of food with you. One would never go into a fine restaurant in New York City, consume a meal, and then expect to walk out of the restaurant and be in Chicago. The same should be true for the in-flight dining experience: As a passenger you are paying for *transport* from here to there, not for the bologna sandwich that we throw in your face. Try to think of the food as a sideshow, not the main attraction. I know the commercials tell you everything is going to be grand, but the truth is that you will be happier if you expect less and bring something of your own, just in case you don't like what we're serving (if we are serving anything at all). Also, most decent airports have improved their concourses and feature a pretty good selection of food. Personally, I try to bring my own food or to eat before I arrive rather than eat the plane food. Naturally, there are exceptions. If you have a close connection or a very long flight you might have to eat what is served on the plane. It won't kill you, but just remember: The flight attendants didn't plan the menu, prepare the food, or forget to put the food on the plane . . . they just serve it! So if you don't like it write a letter to the chef.

This brings me to another thing that has been "eating" at me for some time now; the special-meal protocol. As you may or may not know, airlines offer special meals for those passengers with special dietary needs. You can order them when you purchase your ticket. We don't have them on board unless you order them in advance, and sometimes even then we don't have them. Now, if you order a special meal it means that's what you will be served, it *does not* mean you have a choice of the special meal *or* whatever the unspecial meal is for all the unspecial people on board. Bottom line, you cannot order a vegetarian, kosher, or fruit-plate special meal and then ask if you can also have the regular meal. Sorry, but there's usually only enough food available for each passenger to have one meal.

Sometimes passengers who have ordered special meals try to act as if they are not the special person who ordered the special meal, just so they can have the standard meal. In this case, some poor slob gets stuck eating the liar's special meal or a few bags of lousy peanuts instead of the meal that is rightfully his. This will bring bad karma to you and it is recommended that if you go to the trouble of ordering a special meal that you eat it. Besides, we generally have a list of who ordered what and which seat they've been assigned. In other words, we can find you! I mention this because lately I've noticed an increase in the number of special meals on board; it seems that more and more people are ordering them, only to discover that the standard fare is the better fare. It really is getting out of hand—the other day I had nineteen special meals on board a breakfast flight! The only difference was that the vegetarian meal got peanut butter for the bagel rather than cream cheese. Not very special if you ask me! I think airlines should impose a small surcharge for ordering a special meal; that way only the people who really have to have a special meal would order one. Or better yet, get rid of the meal service altogether—I mean everyone seems to hate the food so much anyhow!

Ah, the meal service is such a chore, and everyone is miserable while it is happening. First of all, the poor passengers cannot get up because the cart completely blocks the aisle. Second, the flight attendant to passenger ratio makes it difficult to serve everyone in a timely manner. Third, it always seems that as soon as we pull the carts into the aisle we hit a patch of surprise turbulence that makes it all the more difficult to pour coffee. In the best interests of the traveling public I have compiled a list of ways that might help make the meal service a bit more bearable, at least for the flight attendants:

1. When ordering a drink—and God knows you'll probably need one after running through the airport, then being stuffed into a metal tube so crowded that it resembles a flying can of sardines, after which you'll be told that you will be sitting on the ground for at least an hour before takeoff—please try to have the exact change, or at least small bills. Once, a woman gave me a twenty-dollar bill for a vodka that cost $4.00 at 7:00 A.M. in the morning. I didn't have the change and could not find it anywhere else, so I suggested she buy four more vodkas and we'd be even. She informed me that if she consumed five vodkas, she'd be drunk as a hoot owl. I pointed out that she didn't have to consume them on the plane during this particular flight. Instead she could take them with her and keep them in her purse. After all, when traveling these days you never know when you might need a little nip. She thought

that was a wonderful idea and gave me another twenty and bought ten bottles. I'm sure this type of salesmanship is contributing to the downfall of our national moral character, selling people things that they don't need and that have an adverse impact on the individual, but sometimes it's every man for himself. I've also had people give me a big bill, say a fifty, and I've had to take a few moments to go locate their change. If I'm not back in ten minutes they start inquiring as to my whereabouts with the other flight attendants. "Where is the brown-haired stewardess, the one in the bad mood? I gave her fifty dollars a long time ago and she hasn't come back." One time I was flying with a real wiseacre and she said, "Oh, you mean Rene. She took your cash and ran out the back door somewhere over Montana."

2. If you're seated next to someone who rings the call button and summons the flight attendant because she'd like a cup of coffee, and you suddenly think that you'd like one too, don't hold it inside! Tell the flight attendant while he is there. Don't be shy, just blurt it right out: "I would like a cup of coffee too, please!" This way he can bring two cups of coffee in one trip. If you wait until he returns and then ask him if you could have a cup of coffee, he may kill you!

3. If you must set your meal tray on the floor because you have to return to your laptop, please have the courtesy to pick up the tray and hand it to the flight attendant when she comes through for garbage collection, rather than making the flight attendant bend down to pick up your dirty tray from the floor.

4. Never tap or poke a flight attendant. I have come home with bruises from passengers poking me in order to get my atten-

tion, even though I am standing there right next to them. One time a gentleman poked me in the rear end in order to get my attention, and I damn near hauled off and hit him. But I refrained and instead poked him back when it was time for me to answer his inquiry. Yes, it is loud on the plane with the engine noise, but most of us can hear and do respond to the following phrases: "Excuse me," "Pardon me," or even the simple "Sir," "Ma'am," or "Miss." There is also that trusty call button located above your seat, right next to the reading light. So, poking or tapping your flight attendant is completely unnecessary.

5. Manners and common courtesy go a long way in an over-crowded airplane. Saying "please" and "thank you" make a world of difference, and you'd be surprised how many people neglect their importance.

6. When walking about the cabin it is advisable to wear your shoes. Especially if you are taking a trip to the lavatory. I have seen a great many people going in there barefoot. I'd like to state for the record, particularly for all of you who practice this disgusting habit, that the fluid on the floor in the bathroom isn't always water, if you know what I mean.

7. If you are interested in "seconds" (hard to believe, but true), wait until everyone on the plane has had "firsts."

The last thing I'd like to remind people is that the flight attendants, just like waiters, are the last ones to touch your food or beverage before you consume it. Keep this in mind at all times and *bon appétit!*

Summer Sale

FOUR YEARS HAD PASSED and by now, Bitsy and I had acquired a little more seniority and a bit more panache. We considered ourselves real New Yorkers and had a scam going with the studio: We had different people coming and going and had almost reduced our rent to nothing. Not only that, but we were starting to enjoy the free travel benefits. I'd taken some pretty fancy vacations to Greece, Paris, Rome, and Frankfurt, and felt, well, very cosmopolitan. Bitsy, too, was becoming quite well known in certain New York social circles and was being invited to some pretty swanky affairs. Of course, it was always a problem trying to bring a date home. I mean, first I had to drag him into a one-room apartment, which is bad enough, but when I arrived at our one-room apartment, I never quite knew what to expect. There might be someone washing her uniform in the bathtub (saves on dry-cleaning), or there might be another couple on the futon already in the middle of a romantic moment, or you could walk in to find four women sprawled out asleep at 8:30 on a Saturday night because they all had a 4:00 check-in the following morning. In any case it was always a surprise and usually a lot of fun, plus it was a good way to get a character reading on your date. The guy could either roll with the punches or he couldn't, and we had no use for the poor chaps who couldn't.

However, some of the happiest times I recall were when it was just us girls sitting around, drinking coffee in the morning, rehashing the events of our latest trips. There were always the common complaints like late flights, full flights, canceled flights, and so forth. Then there were more dramatic occurrences, like when a flight attendant came to work for her India trip with a small cut on her finger, and after working in the germ-ridden galley for a few hours she began to notice that her thumb was turning red and was about three times its normal size. In addition to that she was running a fever, and then she noticed a red streak running up her arm. The crew paged for a doctor, and the only doctor on board was a Japanese man who spoke very little English. There was another passenger who was available to act as a translator, and by then the flight attendant was lying down on the floor of the cockpit, into which were crowded the Japanese doctor and an Indian passenger who spoke Indian, Japanese, and English, as well as the three pilots trying to fly the plane. The doctor had given her some sort of fast-acting antibiotic that he just happened to have in his carry-on luggage. The captain was trying to determine if an emergency landing was necessary, but it was decided that the antibiotic was working well enough to land as scheduled and take the flight attendant to the emergency medical clinic in the airport. By now her thumb was swollen as big as a grapefruit and it was very tender, but her fever was gone and the red streak was disappearing. Upon arrival in India the Japanese doctor escorted the flight attendant to the clinic, which was really just a room next to customs that had an old-fashioned faded yellow curtain that pulled closed, offering the illusion of privacy. It was there that the Japanese doctor informed the Indian translator, who in turn informed the flight attendant, that the doctor would now perform a procedure to release the "poison." With that the doctor pulled out a sharp, blunt instrument that resembled an ice pick—in fact, we believe it was an ice pick. "Hey, wait, aren't you going to, like, clean that thing first?" cried the flight attendant. "You can't just jab a dirty ice pick into my thumb, and you gotta give me something to numb my hand. It hurts just to look at it, let alone stab it!" There was a lot of conversation between the doctor and the translator, but the final verdict was that our suffering flight attendant must "bear the pain."

"Hey, this is the nineties, and people don't bear pain anymore. Tell him I don't want to bear the pain. I'll wait until I get back home, thanks just the same, man!"

The doctor agreed to sterilize the ice pick and after doing so he approached his victim, who was feeling a bit woozy and being held up by the Indian translator, with great precision. Without warning he plunged the ice pick into the wounded, tender thumb. A sudden, piercing cry, which was rumored to be heard at the Taj-Mahal, followed the procedure. As you can see, being a flight attendant is not a career choice for the faint of heart.

Not every story was so dramatic, and sometimes they had not been experienced firsthand, but had just been heard about from someone else or read about in the newspaper. For example, you've probably heard the one about the pig; yes, pigs do indeed fly, and first class at that! The story goes that someone brought along their hog for a trip. He wasn't just any ordinary hog, though, he was a "therapeutic companion"—sort of like those assist dogs you might see guiding a disabled person. Because he was considered a service animal and the passenger had a note from the doctor, the pig was allowed to come along for the ride sans cage or restraints. Apparently, the poor pig didn't fare so well on the descent and by the time they were taxiing to the terminal he went bananas and was reported to have run through the cabin squealing, snorting, and trying to bust in on the boys up front. Actually, that doesn't seem all that unusual to me. As a matter of fact, I've seen quite a bit of squealing and snorting on many flights over the course of my career. I guess I've finally come to understand why it is that airline personnel worldwide dread these two words: "Summer Sale."

The Golden Age

THERE IS DEFINITELY an absence of glamour in the airline industry these days, but that wasn't always the case. There was a time (before deregulation, the current hub and spoke system, air rage, and the overall cynicism pervading the industry) when graciousness and gentility reigned. The following is taken from an airline promotional brochure from the 1950s, when the industry was young.

Step up to the red carpet with pride. This is the double-deck Stratocruiser, the height of flight luxury! Your crew is the pick of the airways. Your comfort is catered to with every innovation known to the air age. Cabin temperature and pressure is altitude-conditioned for perfect ease. A new and exciting travel adventure awaits you.

THE LADIES' LOUNGE: Lovely leather walls—completely mirrored. For convenience, the room is divided into two sections with twin dressing tables to keep you "travel-poster" pretty! Another example of luxury.

MEN'S DRESSING ROOM: Mirrored walls, outlets for electric razors, three washbasins, and a dental basin—plus a never-ending supply of hot water. Everything you need to stay fresh and comfortable en route.

BERTHS: Conveniently lighted—wider than the conventional railroad berth—and curtained for privacy. Also we proudly feature Sleeper Seats, made of deep-cushioned foam rubber. Easy-chair comfort with lots of legroom—at night the chair reclines fully to "chaise longue" position for a smooth slumber.

MEMORABLE MEALS: The gleaming galley is completely equipped to serve oven-fresh full-course meals and delicious between-meal snacks. Prepared on board by professional chefs and graciously served by your stewardess. No tipping at any time, of course.

STRATO LOUNGE: Just step down the spiral staircase to the most distinguished club in the world. Beautifully appointed with built-in bar, horseshoe-shaped couch, and circular table. A unique flight experience.

VANDA ORCHIDS FLOWN FRESH FROM HAWAII: Our gift to you in memory of your trip on the Stratocruiser.

Times have certainly changed and you don't have to be a rocket scientist to recognize it. My mother was a flight attendant (or, at the time, an airline stewardess) from 1951 to 1959, when air travel was considered glamorous, exciting, and even elitist. People actually dressed up for their trips. They wore shoes. Back then most people traveled by car, bus, or train, so taking a trip by plane was a special event, and being a stewardess was a special career. In my mother's day, stewardesses wore white gloves and little boarding hats, they learned to serve lobster thermidor tableside on the airplane, and they had to practice the art of polite conversation with one another so they could better communicate with all the sophisticated passengers. You can only imagine my surprise when I began my career in 1985: Instead of wearing white gloves, we're wearing rubber gloves, and instead of learning to serve lobster thermidor tableside, we're learning to put handcuffs on unruly passengers. Instead of practicing the art of polite conversation, we're practicing the art of self-defense in case we encounter air rage!

Not everything was entirely rosy back in her day, though. For example, stewardesses had to quit when they got married or reached the age of thirty-two. Many women hid the fact that they were married in order to keep their jobs. Secret marriages, how intriguing! They also had to wear girdles. In fact, there was a girdle-checker to make sure they were wearing them and there was also a weight-checker. Stewardesses who stepped on the scale and were over the predetermined proper weight were grounded without pay until they lost the weight. Back then stewardesses had to share hotel rooms on layovers, which would be unthinkable in this day and age, and often women were not allowed to apply for the purser position, which paid more and was only available to men. Still, it was a coveted career and my mother had many fond memories of her days as a stewardess. When I was a little girl she told me stories of the interesting people she had met on her flights: Helen Keller, Duke Ellington, and Richard Nixon to name a few. She grew up on a farm in the Midwest during the Depression and didn't have indoor plumbing for most of her childhood, so it's easy to imagine how thrilling it must have been for her to have a career that allowed her to meet those people; to literally get off the farm and travel the world. She also loved the free travel benefits, and took her parents to places they would never have seen otherwise, like Hawaii and New York City.

Because being a stewardess was such a coveted profession in those days, the airlines could afford to be very particular about whom they hired. Around World War II, some of the earliest stewardesses in commercial aviation were required to be nurses. This requirement was most likely influenced by the military presence in the country at that time. By the 1950s the requirement was dropped and the new trend was to hire beautiful, elegant women (there were very few male stewards at this point in history). Apparently the airlines would announce that they were seeking applications via newspapers across the country and then call in qualified candidates for interviews at the headquarters, much like they still do today. In any case that is how my mother, Maxyne, found out about the job. Actually, it was her younger sister, Janice, who saw the advertisement in the newspaper and wanted to apply, but there was a vision requirement and Janice wore glasses. However, Maxyne, with her 20/20 vision and a burning desire to get off the farm, took a strong interest in the idea and decided she would apply instead.

Within three weeks the girls were on a small plane to the main office for an interview—Maxyne dragged her younger sister along for moral support—and neither had ever been on a plane before. As the story goes, the two girls rented a car and drove from the airport to the personnel office, where Maxyne went for her interview while Janice waited in the car. The airlines could afford to have very specific standards for those they hired, and what they wanted was very beautiful women. Unfortunately Maxyne, although very beautiful, had one small flaw: When she was a little girl a dog bit her, leaving a small scar on the left side of the bridge of her nose. It really was barely visible, but the man in the personnel office noticed it. After the interview he told Maxyne that she met all the qualifications, but because of that small scar, he would have to disqualify her from the application process. This sort of thing could never happen today and if it did, certainly no one would give the actual reason. However, back then that is the way things were, so my mother left the office and went back to the car where Janice was patiently waiting.

Naturally both girls were disappointed and probably figured they would end up spending the rest of their lives on the farm milking cows, or teaching school. They returned the car and went back to the airport to catch their flight back home. When they boarded the plane the sky started turning gray and it began to rain, which was sort of appropriate for their moods at the time. The plane took off and began a very bumpy journey westward; about midway through the flight the captain announced that the weather ahead was worse and they would have to turn around and return to the airport. Janice and Maxyne were not quite sure how this would affect them since the next flight out wasn't until the next afternoon at the same time. When they landed on the ground, personnel arranged a hotel reservation and booked them on the same flight home the following day, thus giving them another twenty-four hours in the "big city." They decided it might be fun to go downtown and see the sights. Maxyne wanted to visit the fancy department stores and see all the latest fashions, and Janice wanted to look at the architecture. They decided to each do her own thing and meet back at the bus stop in one hour. While Maxyne was on her way to the fine furs area, she passed by the cosmetics counter, where she overheard a well-dressed woman and a salesman discussing a foundation cream that covered blemishes and made skin look pure and translucent. Suddenly something clicked in her mind and she approached the man as the other woman was leaving. She told him about her experience with the airlines and showed him the little scar. He put a little bit of the cream on her face and the scar disappeared.

Without hesitation my mother purchased a jar of the cream

and then ran to meet her sister at the bus stop. Janice was amazed at how well the cream covered the scar and even more amazed at Maxyne's plan to return to the airline personnel office first thing the following morning. She wanted to go right then but the office would have been closed. In all actuality it was a good plan since their flight was not leaving until the following afternoon and they had nothing else to do until then. So they both agreed it couldn't hurt to take a chance on going back. After all, the man in personnel told my mother she was exactly what they were looking for. Now that the scar was gone, why wouldn't they take her?

When I first heard this story I was amazed by my mother's tenacity. It took courage to go back after she had been rejected, particularly in that day and age when most women just accepted their lots in life and had very few choices—especially when it came to careers. In any case she went back the next day and showed the man how well the cream worked. Between that and my mother's charm she got herself a fine little job with the airline that lasted eight wonderful years. It was a job she would have kept forever, but the airline forced her to quit when she married my dad in 1959.

As a child I heard a lot of stories about the "good ol' days" and one of my favorites is the one about my mother's friend who was a captain. They would try to get on the same flights because they always had so much fun together; one of the things they liked to do was bid trips out to the West Coast. While they were flying they discovered that they passed right over North Dakota, which was my mother's home state. Her pilot friend figured out how he could pass right over the family farm, so they would tell my grandmother in advance what time they would be flying by and my grandmother would stand out in the backyard and wave her dish towel. Then Mom's captain friend would make some kind of crazy announcement like, "We're now flying over the Peace Garden State, North Dakota. If you look out the right side of the aircraft you can see one of the finest women in the state outside her farm, waving her yellow dish towel, sending you her greetings from the farm!" If that happened today someone would probably report them to the FAA or the CIA or AA.

I've read some of my mother's diaries that she kept throughout her career and I find it fascinating that I'm flying some of the same routes that she flew, doing the same hard work she did nearly fifty years ago. The major difference is that back in her era they seemed to have a lot more fun! There seemed to be more camaraderie. Maybe it's because the airlines were smaller back then. Maybe it's because the industry was new then. Or maybe it was just the way my mother told the stories that made it sound as if they all enjoyed their lives so much. Of course, today we still have fun on the job but it seems to be a different sort of fun than they had. I guess you could say this about a lot of things.

Layovers

L IKE I SAID, times have changed. Nowadays air travel is more like a living hell than a glamorous, elegant experience. The airports are overcrowded, as are the flights, people are impatient, and it's next to impossible to provide the service that people expect. Usually there is some type of delay. Recently I was standing behind a man in line at the ticket counter and overheard the following conversation:

MAN: Well, why is the flight delayed?
AGENT: Weather.
MAN: You know I find that hard to believe. The girl who was here before you just made an announcement, not even ten minutes ago, saying it was a mechanical delay. Now I don't think you're being honest with me and I want to know the truth—right now! Is it a mechanical delay or a weather delay?
AGENT: It's both.

I feel sorry for people who have to travel for work. I can't imagine screwing around all day trying to get somewhere for a business meeting. I mean, the travel in itself is daunting enough, and then upon arrival having to go deal with clients or business makes it all worse. No wonder everyone is so miserable when they travel. At least after I've suffered through a twelve-hour day of travel I'm done! I don't have to concern myself with any other business matters because I am on my layover. One of the most treasured aspects of being a flight attendant, in addition to a flexible working schedule, is the layover. I must admit that this career has given me the opportunity not only to meet many different people, but also to visit many different places. Some people bid trips for the layover: "I've never been to Hong Kong and this month we have twenty-four-hour layovers in Hong Kong. I think I'll bid a few, just to see what it's like there." Other people bid their trips according to what days they would like to have off. Certain people may need Mondays and Wednesdays off because they're taking a class; they don't really care what trip they take or where they layover, as long as they have Mondays and Wednesdays off. Some people want to work one-day trips (turnarounds) because they have kids in school and want to be there when their children arrive home. They will fly four turnarounds in a week, leaving at 6:00 A.M. and returning at 2:00 P.M., and never have to spend the night in a hotel. Still others want to fly long trips, such as six-day trips or even nine-day trips, by concentrating all their flying. Then they may be able to have ten or more days off in a row and be able to use one of their free passes to take personal trips.

There is also something else to be said for taking a nine-day international trip. Let's say you have just suffered a bad breakup or you're sick of your surroundings, or maybe just sort of sick of your life. You hop on a plane to Asia, Africa, or Europe and you really don't know what that trip may bring. There's a sense of excitement and intrigue to it all—even if you have to push a beverage cart across the Pacific. When you arrive you're in foreign land and you can be and do whatever you wish. Maybe you'll want to go out with the whole crew, or maybe you'll want to take off and explore on your own. I love going out with the crew and having a big, fun dinner in Dublin or Florence, but I also love walking around the streets of Tokyo at dusk all by myself and being an outsider. I'm making it sound pretty romantic, aren't I? Well, there is another side to it and that's the more common reality of the layover: Usually it takes place somewhere in America. You've worked a twelve-hour day, all your flights were full, and you've now arrived in some city that looks like the city you were in last night, or maybe it was the night before. In any event it's late and you're tired. The hotel van is late, and when it finally arrives, the driver takes you from the airport along an impersonal interstate in an impersonal part of town past all the impersonal chain restaurants at which you'd never really wish to eat, but at this point you're so hungry that even Denny's sounds good. You keep driving and finally pull into the hotel; sometimes it doesn't have an elevator or the elevator doesn't work, so you have to lug your bags up a few flights of stairs to your cell—I mean your room—which is always located as far from the elevator (or stairs) and as close to the ice machine as possible (that must be one of the requirements of the contract between WAFTI and the hotel). Then you try to unlock your door, but the magnetic key doesn't seem to work, so you leave your bags outside the door, trudge back down to the lobby, and stand in line for five minutes because there is only one front desk clerk and two people are ahead of you. At last, it is your turn. The clerk has to dig around for another key, you trudge back to your room and are delighted to discover this key works. You enter the room, and it stinks. They all sort of stink—either they smell stale or of some putrid scent used to try to cover up the stale smell—so you try to open your window and get some fresh air, but no luck. It's bolted shut. It's now going on 11:00 P.M., and your pickup the following day is 8:00 A.M. You peel off your uniform and suddenly realize you haven't eaten in about eight hours, except for a bag of peanuts.

You're famished, so you call room service, but unfortunately room service and the restaurant close at 10:30 P.M. They suggest you visit the vending machine. . . . Looks like you are out of luck in terms of dinner. Well, the exhaustion of the day is setting in and you decide it might be best just to take a hot shower and hit the sack. You could stand to lose a few pounds anyhow. You turn on the water for a few minutes and as you step into the shower you realize it's freezing cold. You let it run awhile longer—conditions do not improve. Finally, you decide to skip the hot shower and just crawl into bed; even the scratchy sheets and hard pillows do not bother you because you are so tired. You set the alarm and drift off to sleep. About two hours later there is someone next door who has decided to turn on the television, *full blast*. You wake up and look at the clock—it is 1:30 A.M. You toss and turn, maybe get up and go to the bathroom, and now even though you're completely beat, you can't get back to sleep. The "What if I oversleep and the alarm doesn't go off?" panic has set in. You try to close your eyes and return to your golden slumber, but you keep tossing and turning and looking at the clock—every hour. You might be getting in twenty-minute naps, but something keeps you from going into deep undisturbed sleep; no REMs tonight. The more you try to fall asleep the worse it gets. Finally, around 5:00 A.M., you doze off into a deep sleep, only to be ripped out of it by the screeching of the alarm announcing that it's 7:00 A.M. and you have to be dressed and downstairs in one hour. You're hoping the hot-water situation has improved, and it has to some degree, but not entirely. You take a lukewarm shower, get back into that polyester get-up, and off you go in search of a decent cup of coffee. By now you know you are truly living in a fantasy world and until you get home a decent cup of coffee is just another pipe dream. It's back on the van and off to the airport; it sort of seems like you never left. Then it is the standard drill: go through security, board the aircraft, do the pre-flight safety check, prepare the cabin and the galley, and brief with the crew just in time for boarding, when another two hundred people enter into your day, asking for pillows, blankets, water for the pills they have to take, and help putting their Winnebagos into the overhead.

A Sky Goddess Speaks

WELCOME ABOARD, SIR, so glad you could join us today. You have seat 4B. Get you a gin and tonic? My pleasure.

Pleasure, my ass. I don't want to make him a gin and tonic, I'd rather watch paint dry. Come to think of it, I don't want to make anyone a gin and tonic, except maybe myself. Actually, that sounds pretty good right now. Well I guess since I can't have one, ol' 4B might as well. I'll just take a good long whiff of it while I'm making it.

Here you go, sir. Oh, you couldn't find room for your carry-on? You're tired of lifting it and you want someone to get it out of your way?

And I guess I'm the lucky someone. I cannot believe my good fortune. Jesus, what has he got in here? A dead body? If this six-foot, 200-pound bruiser can't lift it, how does he possibly think I, five foot four and 110 pounds—all right, 120 pounds— can lift it? I'll probably rip my shoulder out of the socket if I hold it in this position much longer. Well, I'm glad to see that all my hard labor isn't interfering with his enjoyment of his cocktail. He doesn't seem to even mind all my grunting and groaning. The last thing I would want to do is disturb him. I guess things could be worse; I could be married to him. That'd be a real treat: picking up after him, acting interested in his dull stories about his big job at the plant. . . . No, he doesn't work at a plant, let's see what does he do? Probably some sort of job where everyone runs around kissing his ass all day long while he yells at people and probably threatens to fire them, all the while hoping to God that nobody discovers that he has no clue what he is doing. Look at him, a cell phone in one hand, the *Wall Street Journal* in the other, boy does he think he is important. He's probably talking to a dial tone on the other end. I bet he doesn't even know how to read; he's probably just looking at the letters trying to impress everyone around him. I wonder if knows how to tie his shoes yet.

You know, sir, I think this bag is a little big for the overhead. Perhaps I could check it to your final destination?

Better yet, perhaps I could check you to your final destination and put the bag in your seat. The bag would probably be a lot more interesting.

Unacceptable, you say?

I'll tell you what's unacceptable (aside from the size of your bag): your personality! He probably thinks just because he's sitting in first class that he's entitled to be rude to everyone in the world—I'd be willing to bet my right arm he's an upgrade. I wouldn't want to deprive him of the opportunity to be rude. He probably knocked over a few women and children so he could be the first one in line to board. Well, I'm checking this bag, whether Mr. Congeniality likes it or not. I'm not even going to ask any questions. I'm just putting the tag on it and shipping it off. I guess I'll have to drag it to the front door.

Oh, I didn't mean to disturb you. . . . Yes, well, it looks like the only available option is to check it. It sort of exceeds the size requirements.

A little bit like your ego, pal. Oh boy, he's getting up now. Well that got him into action! Probably hasn't moved that fast in years. My, my, look at those muscles. . . . Amazing how he can heave that two-ton bag into the overhead. Just two minutes ago he didn't have the strength. That gin and tonic did wonders for him.

Now, there's no need to use profanity, sir, I'm sure we can . . .

Yep, he's pissed off now; I pretty much ruined his day. I don't suppose it would make the situation any better if I told him about all the people in the world with real problems. No, that's probably beyond his scope. If having to stow his own goddamn suitcase is the worst thing that has happened to him today, I'd say he is doing all right. Maybe I should give him a copy of Elie Wiesel's *Night* for some in-flight reading. Oh, I forgot, he doesn't know how to read. Well, at least that's over. Oh wait, now he's going to pout. Wait until he discovers there isn't a meal on the flight today—that will probably put him right over the edge. I guess I have to pretend that I care and ask his royal highness if everything is "acceptable." Another opportunity to converse with him.

Thanks so much for helping with *your* bag. I'm glad we didn't have to check it. . . . My name?

My name . . . what the hell does he want my name for? It's not like we're going to be buddies. I hope he isn't under the mistaken impression that we're going to be on a first-name basis with each other anytime soon. I've had years of experience in this department; it will really be better if I call him "sir" and he calls me "miss." I mean, after this flight we won't be hanging out or anything like that. In fact, if things work out the way I am hoping we will never see each other again. So why on God's green earth does he need to know my name? He's probably going to write me up. Why me? I'm just standing here, doing my job, risking my chiropractic good health trying to help this brute with his bag. And what do I get for all my troubles? This idiot requesting my name. Maybe I'll just make up a name. . . . My name is Pain and Humiliation. That's it, good ol' Pain and Humiliation Foss. My friends just call me Misery for short.

Oh no, you don't need to apologize. I'm sure you've had a hard day and having to tow that heavy bag of yours around has got to be tiring. . . .

Hard day? I'll give you a hard day . . . my day! Now that is a hard day. Five stops between Chicago and Indianapolis, airplanes of people just like this jackass. And I've got to do the same thing tomorrow and the next day, too. This is one of the worst trips I've ever had in my life, and I just wanted to bear down and get it over with. There I was just trying to do my job . . . serve the Cokes and pick up the garbage, and now suddenly he walks into my life asking me to make him a gin and tonic and stow his bag and give him my name. What did I ever do to deserve this? All I want is a simple life: to do my job, go home, hide under the covers, and watch television until my next god-awful trip. Is that expecting too much out of life? I think not. So why is it that I am constantly subjected to encounters with such utter fools? *Why me?*

Tonight? Well, I'm flattered, but I have an early pickup in the morning and I . . .

God, I hate my life. I don't think I can take much more of this. We haven't even left the ground and he's already asking me out. Next thing you know he'll be inquiring about the Mile High Club.

Who me? What do I do for fun?

Oh, I like to spend time talking to people like you, trying to figure out ways to get out of situations like this. Another fun thing is watching TV. Yep, I watch a lot of TV. It meets all of my emotional needs. Nothing like sitting down by yourself in front of the tube with the dog, a bottle of wine, and a big plate of pasta on a Saturday night. My favorite shows are *Cops, Jenny Jones,* and wrestling. Oh, I'm a big wrestling fan. I would go out on more dates with eligible men like yourself, but there are just so many fabulous programs that I can't afford to miss. Another thing I like to do for fun is the laundry . . . now that is some serious fun! It's more fun than sitting through an evening with someone like you, I'm sure.

Oh, really? One of the best restaurants in Flint. No I can't say that I've ever been there.

Oh, I don't think I can, but you're so nice to offer. Oh yes, I'm sure there's a lot of great nightlife there, but I really have to get to bed early tonight because I have to wake up at 7:00 A.M. Oh, aren't you funny, you won't take no for an answer. . . .

Oh, he's funny all right. Funny as a crutch. I can't recall the last time I met someone so funny or so debonair—usually you have to be at a trailer park or a bowling alley to meet someone of his status. Well, I imagine he'll keep pestering me until I agree to go to the finest restaurant in Flint with him. Maybe if I'm lucky I'll injure myself in the galley, you know slip on the floor and break my neck, and then I wouldn't have to go. I could just tell him I'm busy with my broken neck and have to spend the night in the finest hospital in Flint instead. He couldn't expect me to go out to dinner with a broken neck.

You're right about that, a girl does have to eat. I guess as long as I'm back by a reasonable hour . . . oh well, why not? I accept away, sir. Charlie? OK, Charlie. Oh, me too. I'm really looking forward to it.

I'm looking forward to it about as much as I'm looking forward to paying my taxes or getting a root canal. Oh, I probably deserve this. Somewhere in the past I must have done some dreadful act for which I am now being punished. The agony of it! I must remember this feeling; perhaps I'll be able to use it in my acting work. Maybe someday I'll have to play a character who is desperate and out of all possible options and I will call to mind this day and my new best friend, Charlie. Charlie this, Charlie that, Charlie, Charlie, Charlie, Charlie. . . . How will I ever live through it?

Oh, get you another gin and tonic? I'll be happy to, Charlie. I'll be right back!

Germ War Fare

EVERYBODY HAS A PHOBIA. I know a flight attendant who is scared to death of flying. It's true! She takes a Dramamine before every flight, wears a St. Christopher medal, and avidly watches the Weather Channel. When it gets really turbulent she goes to the cockpit full of questions, and she bids to work near the forward part of the cabin, where the ride is generally more placid. She has been flying for more than twenty years. One of the phobias both Bitsy and I developed was (and continues to be) "germs." When a passenger tries to put a used Kleenex or a dirty diaper in my bare hands I go crazy! First of all, I won't even take it. I simply smile and say, "I'll be right back," then walk away, and if I'm not too pissed off I'll get a garbage bag. I've been like this to some extent my whole life, but when I started flying it got worse. To this day my hands are like sandpaper from washing them so often with that awful airplane soap. For a time I didn't think that soap killed germs, so I got in the habit of taking a little vodka and pouring it on my hands after the meal service. I figure the alcohol is more effective than the soap and it certainly smells better. Besides, the bathroom lines are so long that it can be three hours before you can actually get in there to wash. In the meantime you have to keep reminding yourself, "Don't touch your face, don't rub your eye, don't scratch your nose," and of course that makes your nose start itching like crazy. You can't imagine how thrilled I was when they invented Purell. It has changed my life.

And if you think the food is bad when you're eating it while crammed into your seat next to a big fat guy, try eating it while sitting in the jumpseat right next to the bathroom. There is often a line of people staring at you (yes, ladies and gentlemen, flight attendants do eat) while, with your meal tray balanced on your knees, you try to shovel some slop down your gullet. That is when people usually want to ask you a question: "So is this your regular route?" Or else they want to ask you for a drink: "Can I have another beer?" (He has had only five and needs another one right now, never mind that you haven't had a morsel to eat in the last ten hours.) Meanwhile, the rest of the line is moving in and out of the lavatory. Many a lousy meal has been ruined for me in this fashion. The only thing that can be said for eating your breakfast, lunch, and/or dinner near a lavatory is that it's probably a great way to lose weight.

One time I was strapped into the jumpseat that faces the passengers and the kid in the passenger seat directly across from me threw up right as the plane was landing. He didn't get to the barf bag in time. It was all over the floor in front of me and on my shoes and nylons. I jumped up and screamed (really professional), and I can still remember every gory detail. That was about ten years ago. Lucky for me I had another pair of nylons and another pair of shoes. It's not only the snot and barf that perpetuates my phobia—it's also the air. It might just be my imagination, but it seems as though a lot more people are coughing and sneezing on me these days. Maybe you've heard about this on the news, but the recirculated air is really bad. As I understand it, a certain percentage of fresh air comes into the cabin, but a larger percentage is just stale air that keeps circulating throughout the cabin during the entire flight. I've been told that the cockpit can control the amount of fresh air that's mixed in with the stale air by turning on more packs, but that uses more fuel. So in order to contain fuel costs the airlines encourage the cockpit to limit the amount of packs they use during the flight. Also, there's about zero percent humidity in the cabin (ergo that lovely dry feeling) and those things combined probably account for the reason you feel like crap after a flight of any length.

I've come to believe that flight attendants develop wonderful immune systems because we really have to combat a lot of foreign particles. What doesn't kill you makes you stronger. Bitsy's trouble began when she got called in for excessive sick calls by good ol' June Larson. It seems that Bitsy had exceeded her allotted sick calls for the year and June wasn't too happy with her. She told Bitsy she would have a "watch dependability" in her file.

"But June, there's been a bad flu going around this year and I didn't call in sick at all last year. I can't help that I'm sick. In fact, I think it's amazing that I haven't been sick more often when you consider all the germs we're exposed to on those airplanes. I'm surprised I'm alive."

"Yeah Bitsy, I hear your concerns, blah, blah, blah. Now I want to know what you are going to do to improve your dependability. We can't have people at WAFTI we can't rely on."

"Well, if I'm sick I don't think I should come to work. That would just make everybody else sick. I think if I am sick I should stay home," said Bitsy.

"Sometimes you're so sick you need to stay home, but other times you need to tough it out. Now I don't want you calling in sick the rest of the year. Do you think you can do that?"

"Well, June, I'm not going to make any promises. I'll do my best."

"Super! Now what are you going to do to prevent yourself from getting sick for the rest of the year?" June inquired.

"Frankly, I don't know. I take vitamins, I eat, I sleep, I exercise."

"OK Bitsy, why don't you think of some other things you might do to prevent any more illnesses this year and get back to me."

Needless to say, Bitsy was very unhappy after that encounter with June Larson. It became a running joke—how could we prevent getting sick? Did not calling in sick include accidents? For example, if we were in a car accident and Bitsy broke both her legs, was she expected to come to work? Certainly some people abuse sick time, but Bitsy was a very good employee and really didn't call in sick unless she was sick. I suppose that's what made her so mad about the whole thing. By the time Bitsy ran into June again, she had acquired a plastic eye shield, rubber gloves, a surgical mask, paper shoes, and a gown from a doctor friend of hers. On her next outbound trip, Bitsy put on all the medical garb over her uniform, armed herself with a can of Lysol, and marched into June's office, announcing that she had found a way to prevent any further illnesses for the year. She was quite confident that she would not miss any more trips. June didn't find the whole thing very funny and gave Bitsy a serious reprimand, but to us it was worth it and we kept the costume for a possible Halloween outfit.

Boarding
A Shakespearean Tragedy

T HESE DAYS IT SEEMS that people will almost kill for a first-class seat. I guess it's because conditions are so deplorable in coach. One day I saw two grown adults get into a fight over the last seat in first class. Apparently the computer had made an error (hard to believe, I know) and there were twelve seats but thirteen passengers. Now, we're one of the most civilized, technologically advanced nations in the world, but the behavior of these passengers took me back to the fifteenth century. There is only one word to describe it: "barbaric."

It was a dark and stormy night. There was thunder, lightning, heavy rain, and a full moon. The three flight attendants prepared the galley and checked the meal count, and as they did so they began to chant:

> "Double, double toil and trouble
> Fire burn and cauldron bubble."

"What does thou serve for those who sup in first class?" asked the head flight attendant.

The second answered, "Filet of rattlesnake in the cauldron boil and bake. Wool of bat wrapped in a leaf."

"In other words, chicken or beef," said the third.

A lightning bolt flashed and heavy thunder rumbled. "A

drum, a drum, the passengers doth come," cried the boarding agent.

The first passenger, let us call him Macbeth, boarded.

"How now, you secret, black, and midnight hags! What is 't you do?" he inquired, as he removed his cape and hat.

"A deed without a name. We live to serve," responded the flight attendants.

"Hail Macbeth, hail to thee. Here is your seat, you have 1B. The last remaining in first class. Now give me your cape and your boarding pass."

As Mr. Macbeth got situated in his seat, he heard a strange eerie voice that whispered:

"Macbeth, Macbeth, Beware Macduff
Beware the Thane of Crete
Beware Macbeth, she wants your crown
Beware Macbeth, she wants your seat."

It bothered him that no one else seemed to hear the voice, but he had been working hard and was tired and things weren't going so well with Lady Macbeth back at the castle. The stress was probably getting to him. Maybe he just needed to take it easy and relax he decided, but he would mention this to his doctor on his next visit. At that moment the thirteenth passenger, Ms. Macduff, entered and the flight attendants assumed the position. In unison they chanted:

"Hail, Hail, Hail Macduff
We see thy crown, we kiss thy feet."

"Enough, enough. There is someone in my seat!"

The junior flight attendant came rushing to her aid, "May I see your boarding pass?"

Ms. Macduff shoved it in her face and sure enough it was the same seat assignment.

The junior flight attendant, not knowing what to do and feeling very afraid of Ms. Macduff, ran to the senior flight attendant and whimpered, "Fie, fie, fee, fee. . . . Ms. Macduff also has seat 1B."

"Ah me, toil and trouble, boil and bubble, when seat assignments here are double!" She pulled the junior flight attendant into the galley and tried to decide what type of service recovery would best suit the situation. Meanwhile, the passengers took matters into their own hands—which is always a dangerous thing.

"Pray, kind sir, but you're in my throne, where I shall rest till dawn. Remove thyself and get thee gone," Ms. Macduff proclaimed.

Macbeth, with no intention of leaving his seat, fastened his seat belt and announced, "I'll not move, I'll not fail. Screw my courage to the sticking place, this is *my* seat and this is *my* space!"

Ms. Macduff growled at him.

Well, Mr. Macbeth would not stand for this. It was going to be a long flight to Scotland and he was exhausted from all the battles he had just fought. So he grabbed the toenail clipper that he had stowed properly in the overhead bin and let this broad have it.

> "Fie, fie, I am a frequent flier.
> I'll not share this seat with
> The likes of you, a common liar."

Ms. Macduff was insulted, and not being one to back down she set down her cell phone, grabbed her eyelash curler, and countered:

"What care I how much you fly?
I am in the Regal Club and
Have a private room at every hub."

By now the two of them were standing in the aisle lunging and parrying about the cabin. The flight attendants hid in the galley and the other passengers took cover. Macbeth jumped onto the seat.

"Ha! I own the stock, I am the board
When I arrive, they call me Lord."

Ms. Macduff, with her eyelash curler in hand, inquired,

"Lord of what? Pray do tell.
Lord of this? Me thinks it hell."

You have to admit she had a valid point. However, Macbeth's adrenaline was racing and he wasn't about to give into this shrewish hellhound. He shouted at her:

"Nonetheless, that is my seat and it I shall defend.
You, poor wench, will ride in back with all the common men."

He jumped down from the seat and let out a mighty roar and an evil guffaw as Ms. Macduff fell forward with despair at the very thought of it.

"Ride in coach? I'd rather ride in a boat."

With that a full-fledged battle ensued. Passengers were taking cover, while the flight attendants continued trying to serve drinks. Accidentally, the junior flight attendant got caught in the fray while trying to bring Mr. Macbeth a nice cold beer. The beer fell off the tray onto Ms. Macduff's brand-new Anne Klein suit. This stopped the action, and Macbeth said to the flight attendant,

> "You wench, you fool,
> You've spilled my beer
> I'll write your boss and
> Ruin your career."

The flight attendant began to furiously scrub the stain on Macduff's suit. "Out, out damn spot . . . ," she sobbed. The head flight attendant ran to her assistance, offering her a tip she had learned from years and years of flying: "A little bit of club soda will take that right out, honey." With that they threw a can of club soda on Ms. Macduff. Then before Ms. Macduff could react they hobbled back to the galley, muttering to each other, "Fie, fie, fee, fee, how are we to serve amidst all this clatter?" At that moment Ms. Macduff pulled a curling iron from her carry-on and thrust it into Macbeth's soft belly. With a chilling laugh she declared, "I've got you now, size doth not matter."

Macbeth fell from his first-class seat to the floor. And without missing a beat, Ms. Macduff sat down in seat 1B, for which she had battled valiantly and fairly won. And then suddenly, just as she began to relax, Mr. Macbeth, in a surprising come-back, pulled out a golf club from under the seat in front of him. He screamed, "It matters not!" as he whacked Ms. Macduff in the head. He fell backward just as Macduff fell forward on top of him.

When the head flight attendant came out of the galley to begin the cleanup process, she looked about and commented:

"Dead, dead, me thinks them dead
Beer has been spilled, body fluid shed.
And yet here lies a seat that is free and
For this chance other beggars outside do
Wait, spewing forth and bitching at the gate.
So bring them in, the next of kin and seal the
Final fate."

At that moment, during the trumpet fanfare, in sauntered a young man, Mr. Hamlet. He was very well dressed, but looked a bit preoccupied with his own thoughts. As he entered he said out loud, "To be or not to be? That is the question, whether 'tis . . ."

"No, no, no!" said the head flight attendant. "Excuse me, Mr. Hamlet? Not 2B . . . 1B . . . right over here."

To Sleep, Perchance to Dream

S OME PEOPLE ARE JUST naturally happy. They see the glass as being half full rather than half empty, even when there is nothing in the glass! They are cheerful and friendly and nothing rattles their cages. They have ready smiles, they're approachable, and I have no idea how they got that way. Perhaps they were born that way, but whatever the case . . . there they are and I loathe them.

Recently I was on a flight at 6:00 A.M., traveling as a passenger to my annual training. Along with all the other passengers, I wanted one thing and one thing only—to sleep. The sun had not yet come up and the cabin lights had been dimmed. The plane had taken off and I was completely out when all of a sudden a bolt of sound coming through the public address system ripped me out of my tranquil slumber.

"Good morning, ladies and gentlemen. This is Captain Pete P. Peters, your pilot, and I want to personally welcome you aboard flight 555 to Paducah. We pushed out of Poughkeepsie promptly and are proceeding to our position. Here at WAFTI we're pretty proud of our ability to predict patterns and progressions of weather points. Our flight promises to be smooth, so sit back and relax."

Finally, he was finished, but just as I began to doze again came this: "We're pleased to have some of the industry's most professional personnel and today I am pleased to present Paula, Peggy, and Penelope—your flight attendants! They're here primarily for your safety, but your comfort is another priority. These gals are not only personable, poised, punctual, and polite, but they are also pretty darn good-looking. Let them know if you need anything. I'll be back later to pass on some points of interest."

Just my luck I get on the plane with the captain who really wants to be a radio announcer. Well, there isn't much more he can possibly say. I know my fellow passengers shared my sentiments because there was a collective groan when yet again the happy voice came bounding out of the speakers: "Pete P. Peters here again! Just want to give you a progress report. Today we will be passing over some popular and prominent parts of our nation: Pittsburgh, Petersville, and Peoria. You probably didn't know this but Peoria is a leading producer of petunias. I'll point that out when we get a little closer in case anyone wants to take a picture of Peoria's petunias."

Noooooooooo! Why is this happening to me? All I want to do is sleep. I don't think I can tolerate it for the next three hours. Maybe it's mind control. It's one thing to be given information, but this is more than I want to know! We passengers want to sleep—what is Pete P. Peters trying to prove with all these PAs? Does he feel that since he has to be awake so does everybody else? Perhaps he is the sleep police and he has to be sure that nobody gets more than ten seconds of sleep. I am so exhausted, but suddenly there is a jolt and the plane seems out of control.

"Pete P. Peters here and we've got some pretty potent turbulence. I apologize that we can't always project this. That's one of my pet peeves about being a pilot! Don't panic folks because these planes can really pack a punch! It's our policy never to put our passengers in a precarious position. I would like to have Paula, Peggy, and Penelope sit down just to be safe and . . ."

The next thing we heard was a lot of rumbling over the PA system. There were two voices, but you could not make out what they were saying. Meanwhile the plane seemed to be careening out of control. The passengers were hanging on for dear life. Then, as suddenly as it came upon us, the turbulence was gone. The ride was smooth and the cabin quiet. Maybe now I could get some shut-eye. I closed my eyes. I relaxed my muscles. I took a deep breath, and then: "Ladies and gentlemen, this is First Officer John Smith. Don't be alarmed, but I've just killed Pete P. Peters."

The cabin broke into applause and cheers. Some passengers were yelling, "Bravo!"

"His incessant chatting was keeping everyone awake, including me! So rest assured you won't be hearing any more pesky PAs from perky Pete P. Peters!"

I finally fell into a deep sleep. It seemed that the silence was a gift from God. I was just starting to dream when another voice came over the PA. This time it was nasal and high-pitched, with a Southern accent.

"Good morning, ladies and gentlemen, this is Peggy. Penelope and Paula will begin the breakfast service now. You may have pancakes with peach preserves or a poppy-seed muffin. We also have peanuts and pretzels. If you'd like to join us for breakfast please lower your tray table. If it's not lowered we will not serve you because we don't want to disturb anyone who is possibly trying to sleep. Thank you."

Dr. Love

AFTER MORE THAN five years of living on the Upper East Side of Manhattan, Bitsy and I decided it was time for a change of scenery. We found an adorable apartment in Greenwich Village. We didn't have as many people passing through because we were now making a bit more money. Good thing, because having all those people in and out of the apartment was tiring, not to mention confusing. So, it was basically two chicks from the Midwest living in the Village. Whenever people discovered that Bitsy and I were single flight attendants living in New York City they always wanted to know about our love lives. Frankly, I didn't see the logic in their line of questioning. I guess some people are still under the impression that being a flight attendant is like it was in the 1960s—you know, "Coffee, tea, or me?" or "Marry me, fly free" (nowadays it's "Marry me, fly standby"). I suppose some people think I'm out there jet-setting around the world meeting rich, handsome, sophisticated men. They must think that I'm partaking in innumerable sexual escapades in exotic locations. Unfortunately, nothing could be further from the truth. No, if someone were to write a cable television show about my life it would not be called *Sex and the City* but *NO SEX and the City* (or anywhere else for that matter). Of course, I would be lying if I told you that I never, ever indulged in a little fling. But for the most part it seems that men these days are far too plugged in to their cell phones, laptops, and other electronic devices to pay much attention to the gal picking up the garbage on an airplane (that's me). However, every now and again some poor slob's battery is run-down and he believes it's the job of "trash girl" to recharge it. How do I recognize this poor bastard? He usually makes a feeble attempt at a joke, like "How do I get to be a member of the Mile High Club, baby?" Of course, there's no such club any longer; it went the way of glamour, civility, and manners, but I, as a safety and service professional, must treat all my passengers with the dignity and respect they deserve, no matter how twisted they may be. For that I deserve a huge raise! I politely answer the question and try to get the hell away from the jerk as soon as possible.

Now it can also work the other way. There may be someone on the plane that you think you would like to meet. The operative word here is "think," because if you do in fact meet him, in the end, he is never what he appears to be. This phenomenon often applies to meeting people on the ground as well. It seems, for me anyway, that the men I like never like me and I never like the men who like me. There have been a lot of books written on this very subject—I know, because Bitsy and I have read many of them: *Women Who Love Too Much; Men Are from Mars, Women Are from Venus; Women Men Love, Women Men Leave.*

Personally, I think someone should write a book and call it *Women Men Never Approach in the First Place.* I suppose you're thinking, "This girl has no faith in relationships." Well, you're right. I had reached a point where I had given up dating. It's so god-awful, going out on a date, especially with someone you've met on a plane. One minute you're showing him how the oxygen mask works and then, bang, he's proposing marriage. And what's even worse is a blind date. There aren't many things you can count on in life, but there are a few . . . like death, taxes, and the fact that Rene Foss will never go out on a blind date ever again! You see, when you go out on a blind date it's because someone thinks you'd be a perfect match for this loser friend of hers. Most of the time I would prefer to stay home and do the laundry, but because your best pal or cousin or fellow employee thinks you "have to" meet her dear friend Mr. Jukes because "you'd be sooooo perfect together," you reluctantly go on this date. They think they're doing you a big favor and that you should be grateful to them for it. I'm ashamed to admit that I got to a point where I would go on a blind date only if I was a little low on cash and needed a free meal. But I've even given that up now because I'd rather have Kraft Macaroni and Cheese six nights a week than suffer through one more painfully dull date with a stranger, both of us trying to generate conversation, trying to act like we're having a good time, and, worst of all, secretly hoping that this might work out, only to discover thirty minutes into the date that it will never work, not in a million years, and then having to spend the next two or three hours together. I would rather be alone and single for the rest of my days, thank you very much.

So I became a confirmed spinster, and proud of it! I even began a tradition with some of my "old maid" friends called the Spinster's Dinner. Every year during the Christmas holidays we get together at the Head Spinster's home and celebrate. We all wear black, give one another used gifts in a Yankee Swap fashion, and have a delicious meal of seafood linguini, salad, wonderful homemade bread, and lots of wine! No men allowed and no married women either! It is a very exclusive, special club. In any case, Bitsy was beginning to worry about my preoccupation with spinsterhood: "Do you really believe you're never going to get married?" she asked me one day.

"Bitsy, I never even think about it."

"Yes, but you're so young, and here you are living in a fabulous city with millions of men in it. Not to mention all of the traveling. You have to admit there are some men on our flights that aren't so bad. I think you're giving up too quickly." She was pushing me.

"Look, Bits, I'm very happy. Why should I start going out and screw it all up?"

"I'm just saying that you should not rule out the possibility of ever going out on a date again. Maybe your standards are too high."

"Are you saying that I should lower my standards?"

"Well, yes. In a way I have."

"Yeah, I know. Your only standard is that he be male."

This was sort of the truth. Bitsy, God love her, would go out with anyone who had the guts to ask. She believed it was a numbers game: The more you go out the more you increase your chances of meeting Mr. Right. However, there was one huge flaw in her plan: You had to go out with a lot of freaks, and as a flight attendant living in New York you have the opportunity to meet all kinds. Here are some of the men we dated between the two of us, many of whom we met on flights: convicts, illegal aliens, men who wanted to be women, doctors, lawyers, unemployed actors, men born with silver spoons in their mouths, men with silver spoons in their noses, washed-up rock stars from the late 1970s, airline pilots, flight attendants, musicians, young men, old men, poor men, rich men, rich old men with bad coughs, men we loved who left and men we did not love who would not leave, Italians, Greeks, Albanians, scene partners from acting class, men who wear leather driving gloves in the summer—and this was all before I reached the age of twenty-five. Many people want to know if I've ever had a serious, long-term relationship, and I often answer, "Oh yes, of course, and it was the greatest night of my life."

During that same period of time I did start dating someone

(I guess Bitsy's pep talk did have some influence on me). He was a gynecologist—not mine, but a gynecologist nonetheless. We met on a flight and it turns out that Dr. Love and I had some common interests. For one thing, we were both taking tap-dance classes in New York. We started talking about it and before you know it he was asking me to dinner and a show. I was a little sick of macaroni and cheese so I agreed to go with him. Actually, we had a great time and it was fun to be with him. And the fact that he was a doctor led me to believe he was stable and could possibly be "marriage material."

At first it didn't bother me that he was a medical doctor who wanted to be an actor-dancer. I mean, I was a flight attendant who wanted to be an actress, but eventually it did seem a little odd and then it began to irritate me. One minute he was delivering babies and the next he was auditioning for *Gypsy*. I can't imagine my gynecologist back home practicing Broadway show tunes in between pap smears. I began to wonder if Dr. Love was marriage material after all. One day he called me and said that he only wanted to date until the end of the summer and then we should probably break up. Let's say in September. Now, I've gone out with plenty of men, but in all my born days I have never heard that one. I mean usually people don't schedule their breakups. I began to wonder if maybe he was already married to someone who was away for the summer and would be returning in the fall. Maybe I was just a summer fling. I wondered if it was some kind of sick joke, but then I stopped wondering and was really pissed. After a few more weeks I began to feel that if we were going to break up in September we might as well break up now, in July. That way there would be less to forget and I could get over the pain quicker. I mean, why drag it out if it's going to be over soon anyway? So one night while preparing my macaroni and cheese, I called Dr. Love and told him it was over. He couldn't understand why and tried to change my mind, but I stuck to my guns. I was a little sad for about two minutes, but then I bounced back and was ready to move on to the next chapter of my life. Three weeks later the doctor called again, "Hey darlin', how are you? I was wondering if you would like to get together this weekend for a drink?" he asked.

"Why?" I answered. In my mind this was a done deal and already over by the Fourth of July.

"Well, Rene, I'd like to see you. I miss you," he said in a soft voice, trying to be sweet and sexy.

My response to him? "Pretend it's September."

I didn't date another passenger for a long time after that fiasco. The only thing worse than dating a passenger is dating a pilot, but that's another chapter entirely.

I Hate Everything

THE SCENE: A crowded airplane. Delayed flight out of major East Coast city. It's Friday afternoon, there's a sense of chaos in the air. In seat 7B sits an uptight man, mid-thirties. He's had a bad day. His investment portfolio is not doing well, he had a fight with his boss, and he didn't sleep well the night before. His demeanor brings to mind that of an agitated bull.

ENTER: A stressed-out businesswoman, dressed in black and carrying a leather bag with her laptop and piles of papers that overflow the bag. She is barking into her cell phone: "That is *not* acceptable and you better have it straightened out by Monday. I don't care if it takes you all weekend!" She is looking for her seat.

WOMAN: Is that seat 7A? (pointing to open seat next to the window)
MAN: I guess so.
WOMAN: I asked for an aisle seat. Are you sure you're in the right seat?
MAN: Positive.
WOMAN: I hate this airline; they can never do anything right.

She throws her bag on to the floor and then plops down in a big huff next to the agitated bull.

WOMAN: God, I hate flying. Don't you hate flying? Look at how crowded it is, everyone is flying.

Someone coming down the aisle bangs the man's head with an oversized piece of carry-on luggage.

MAN: Ow, watch it, pal.

The other passenger, unaware of his transgression, looks at him and apologizes bewilderedly.

MAN: Don't you hate people? Dumb clumsy people. God, I hate people.
WOMAN: Yeah, I hate people.
MAN: Are you gonna keep that bag there the entire flight?
WOMAN: I don't know. Are you going to keep your shoes off the entire flight?
MAN: None of your business. Yup, I really hate people. (He glares at her.)

They remain in their own worlds until after takeoff. The flight attendants are now coming through the aisle with their beverage carts.

WOMAN: Finally, we're going to get something to drink around here.
MAN: Yeah, it's about time.
F/A: Care for something to drink, sir?
MAN: Yeah, I'd like a nice cold beer.
F/A: Yeah, so would I. . . . Here. (She slams it down.)

Man sips beer. It's warm.

MAN: Jesus! Don't you hate warm beer?
WOMAN: Served with such great cheer?
MAN: What's there to like here?
WOMAN: Nothing at all . . .
WOMAN: I hate Pepsi, I hate Coke,
　　　　And people who can't take a joke.
　　　　I hate Starbucks, I hate pearls,
　　　　I hate boys who want to be girls,
　　　　I hate weekend coffee clutch,
　　　　I hate HMOs so much,
　　　　I hate flying on a jet,
　　　　and I hate the Internet!
　　　　God, I really hate my job,
　　　　TV shows about the mob,
　　　　Bottled water, sushi too,
　　　　Oprah's book club
　　　　How 'bout you?
MAN:　　I can't stand yuppies or soft, fluffy puppies.
　　　　Hate New York City, humor that's witty.
　　　　God, I hate tofu, Jerry Seinfeld, Leno, Letterman,
　　　　Star Wars, too.
WOMAN: You really hate Letterman?
MAN: Yeah, I really do.
WOMAN: I've never met anybody who hates Letterman. . . .
　　Everybody else loves him.
MAN: I can't stand all that . . .
WOMAN: Hype?
MAN: Yeah . . . hype.
WOMAN: Speaking of hype, what about the Oscars?
MAN: The worst!
WOMAN: You know what I really hate?
TOGETHER: Technology.

WOMAN (Quite surprised): We hate the same things.

MAN (Bewildered): That's the strange thing.

WOMAN: Let's see what this can bring, hating the same things.

A shy smile begins to come across her face.

WOMAN: I hate Sprint, it makes me cry.

MAN: I hate cell phones.

WOMAN: So do I! (She throws hers down the aisle.)

MAN: I hate junk mail, I hate quiche, and I hate the nouveau riche.

WOMAN: People who do not call back, and I hate the Nordic-Track.

MAN: Media bombarding me.

WOMAN: Crappy talk shows on TV.

MAN: We hate everything it seems.

WOMAN: Still we hold on to our dreams!

TOGETHER: The world is full of things we do not love, but there's one thing I know is true: I could love hating life with you!

They kiss passionately. A flight attendant passes by and throws a blanket over them.

F/A: God, I hate love!

My Brilliant Career
in Daytime Drama

O
K, I'VE BEEN GOING on and on about how I wanted
to be an actress, but it was certainly not easy for me. I
can't figure out if it was because of the job and the fact
that I was away so much or because I have no theatrical ability
whatsoever. But let's put it this way, except for a few little things
here and there, I was nowhere near being an actress. In fact, the
only acting I was doing was acting like I cared about all the troubles at WAFTI—for that I could win an Academy Award. However, I'm not one to give up too quickly. I continued to go on
auditions, attend classes, and get new head shots, all while flying
my scheduled trips.

One day on a flight there was a passenger who looked very
familiar to me. At first I thought I might have dated him, but that
wasn't it and then suddenly, in the middle of picking up the
garbage, it hit me. He was an agent and I had auditioned for him
about three months before. He was casting small roles on soap
operas. I had read for the part of a reporter and obviously did not
get the job. Anyway, there he was—this casting director, right
there in 17B. I didn't know quite how to handle this. Even
though I remembered him, he didn't seem to recall me. I wasn't
sure if I should approach him or just forget the whole thing. On
one hand it might be a wonderful opportunity to remind him of
my great potential as an actress and maybe even get another

appointment to audition for him. On the other hand, I was wearing a polyester pantsuit, very little makeup, and my hair was in an ugly ponytail. Not to mention that I had been on duty for ten hours. I wasn't exactly projecting an image I would like to have etched in this man's mind.

After a lot of hemming, hawing, and discussion with the crew I decided to go for it. He looked bored and if he seemed annoyed I wouldn't bother him. I'd just stop by and say hello and go from there. Before I did anything I hit the lav with its flattering fluorescent light and tried to reassemble myself into something that didn't look so much like a creature from *Night of the Living Dead*. It wasn't easy, but I managed. I sauntered up the aisle to 17B, where I found Mr. Casting Director immersed in a script.

"Hi. I am so sorry to bother you, but I think I may know you."

"Oh?"

"Yes, I believe we met a few months ago at your office. Aren't you a casting director?"

What a dumb thing to say! In my mind I'm always so smooth and articulate, but in reality I always manage to say really dumb things and that has to be one of the dumbest things I have ever said. "Are you a casting director?" What kind of an idiot am I? I realized that I should have just stayed in the galley, reading my *People* magazine like a good little flight attendant, but no, I had to go out and try to network. Dumb! Well, it was too late now. I tried to weasel my way out of it as gracefully as possible.

"Yes, I am. Were you in for an audition?"

"As a matter a fact I was. I was reading for the part of the reporter."

"Right. Well, the writers cut that reporter out of the show, so it turns out we didn't hire anyone for the job."

Hey, this was going a lot better than I'd thought. He was really nice and seemed pleased that I approached him.

"I hate flying," he continued.

"So do I."

We both laughed at that one. Then we reintroduced our-selves and began to chat about the show, auditioning, and flying. After a few minutes of chatting he gave me his card and asked me to call him on Monday because there was another audition and I might just be perfect for the part. I almost fell over. Need-less to say I took the card and promised to call. I could hardly stand the weekend, I just wanted it to be Monday so I could call Mr. Casting Director. When Monday finally came around I made the call and he asked me if I could come in for a cold reading early Tuesday morning. Could I come in for a cold reading? What kind of a question is that? Could I come in for a cold read-ing? Ha. OF COURSE I COULD COME IN FOR A COLD READING!

To me this was the big time, because in terms of soaps, I had never really gone any further than being a "supporting player," which really means an "extra." I knew this was bigger than that because he wanted me to read for him. Supporting players do not read for things. Maybe it was for a regular character on the show. Maybe they were writing in a new character and it had "me" writ-ten all over it. I wondered if it was the ingénue, maybe the romantic lead . . . maybe not. Maybe it's the slut—I'll bet it's the slut! I've always wanted to play a slut. It'd be such a stretch!

I went in on Tuesday, about twenty minutes early so I could review the material and have a few extra moments to prepare. The receptionist gave me the script and I began to read. The scene was taking place on an airplane. The basic gist was there is a couple on a private jet, sneaking off to a romantic getaway. They're having a very elegant dinner when suddenly the plane loses control. This seems very dramatic so I'm beginning to won-der if I can pull off the elegance and the drama when suddenly the words "ENTER FLIGHT ATTENDANT" pop off the page. Oh no! I've now made the sad realization that they don't want me for the lead, they want me for the flight attendant.

It's not really a "sad" realization because I'm truly thrilled to be considered for anything. But gee whiz, a flight attendant? The one thing from which I'm trying to escape, and I get my one big chance and bang . . . there it is staring me in the face yet again! All of a sudden Mr. Casting Director is standing in the doorway. "Hi! Nice to see you again. I'm glad you had a chance to look over the script. I thought it was so appropriate for you, I mean, you'd certainly be able to bring some reality to the role, if you're selected." He was smiling and I certainly didn't want to project or reveal any disappointment. After all, the part of the flight attendant had a lot of dialogue, it was two days' work, and the scene was very dramatic. So what if I wasn't the lead? All I had ever done up to this point was extra work, so this was a big step forward in my career.

"Oh, I think it's ingenious on your part! If I can't play this role correctly then I'm really in trouble," I said, with a big flight-attendant smile on my face.

"Well, terrific! Let's get started."

And with that I gave one of the best auditions of my life and left. Three hours later Mr. Casting Director called me at home and told me I had gotten the job. Wow! I was to pick up the script the next day and the taping would be the following Monday at the television station. Flight attendant or not, I must admit I was pleased.

I picked up the script and began to memorize the lines and think about the scene. It wasn't exactly true-to-life in terms of commercial air travel, but since it was set on a private jet it was a bit more believable. The day of the big taping I was to report to the television station at 7:00 A.M. to do a read-through with the other actors and then a rehearsal with the director. I was there early and when the actors came in for the read-through, I was really excited. They were so nice to me and made me feel comfortable. They were also very impressed with my knowledge of the script. I had not only memorized all *my* lines but I had also memorized *their* lines. Any time they forgot a line I had it right on the tip of my tongue and would just throw it out to them and for that they seemed grateful. The rehearsal with the director went well and then it was on to hair and makeup, one of my favorite things in life. First of all, I adore the attention. About five people descend upon you, sort of sizing up your potential, and then they go to work. In about an hour you look like a million bucks! I didn't even recognize myself. I was so delighted with the way they made me look that I called Bitsy and said I wanted to meet her for lunch somewhere very chic because I looked so fabulous!

Finally the time had come for the taping of the actual scene. I was a little nervous because I didn't want to make a mistake, but as soon as I entered the set I could see that it was a pretty laid-back atmosphere. Everyone was joking and laughing and very friendly. Also, word had gotten out that I was a *real* flight attendant and everyone wanted to tell me horror stories from recent flights. Sometimes being a flight attendant is a terrific icebreaker, if you can stand hearing everyone's war stories over and over.

The set was incredible. They had an actual mock-up of an airplane, with all the accoutrements, such as meal carts, china, crystal, real food that looked delicious, and even champagne (I told you it wasn't like commercial air travel, but hey, it's television). As I mentioned earlier, the plane suddenly lurches out of control because the pilot passes out, and then the handsome hero has to save the day by taking over the controls and safely landing the plane. I thought this was a bit of a cliché, and in my humble opinion, the flight attendant should have landed the plane. However, this was not the case, so I thought it was best to just go along with the program. I was very curious about how they would make the plane lurch and create the necessary turbulence for the scene to seem real, and then I noticed that the plane had a long pole underneath it and the whole contraption sat on inner tubes. When it was time for the turbulence three guys on the left and three guys on the right would move the long poles back and forth and actually rock the plane on the inner tubes. The effect was quite realistic, especially when you were moving about on the plane trying to carry a tray. The time for the first take had arrived and the director called "Action," and we began the scene.

"Good evening, Mr. Winters, welcome aboard!"

Then there were a few lines about what they would be having for dinner when suddenly the plane careens left then right. I had to act like I was in control, but also show that I was a bit frightened. Frankly, I felt like laughing every time it happened but, being the consummate acting professional, I restrained myself.

"What the hell is going on?" inquired the character of Mr. Winters.

"I don't know, I'll check with the pilot," I replied, and then ran to the cockpit.

When my character returned Mr. Winters wanted a full explanation of what was happening and I told him that the pilot had passed out.

"Well, then who is flying the plane?" Mr. Winters demanded to know.

And then I got to deliver one of the best lines of my life: "No one is flying the plane!"

With that the plane lurched again and I almost started to laugh out loud, but I stayed in character and continued with the scene. It went on like this for a while, with a few retakes here and there. In the final moments of the scene, the hero safely lands the plane while I tend to the pilot. I leave the cockpit to get a cold cloth and never return—typical flight attendant.

And that, ladies and gentlemen, was my big television debut. Maybe you saw it. I thought for sure they would be calling me again with other parts, bigger parts, but no such luck. The next time they called—about a year later—it was for a smaller part, an extra. I accepted it, of course, but with definite disappointment. Realizing how unstable show business could be I was actually beginning to feel gratitude for my father's words of wisdom about *benefits*. I was a bit of a celebrity around the airline for a while. "Oh, hey, weren't you the one on the soap opera?" people would ask me. That was fun, but it passed rather quickly and then I was back to being a nobody in a blue polyester uniform again.

Getting Off the Ground

I T STARTED WITH JUST a few deceptive flakes on Sunday morning, but by late afternoon the entire metropolitan region was getting pummeled with sleet, snow, high winds, flooding, and even thunder and lightning. The forecasters predicted blizzardlike conditions and the governor had even declared a state of emergency. Schools were closed, and the National Guard was called in to protect citizens. The employees at the Weather Channel were on twenty-four-hour high alert; a good old-fashioned northeaster was on the way. They were calling it the Winter Blitz, and the best part was that I had a rotten three-day trip scheduled to depart at 6:00 A.M. Monday morning. I was brimming with joy because I was positive my flight would be canceled, and I would be able to get out of the trip. Whoopee! Here it was Sunday afternoon and most of the major airlines were already canceling all flights for Monday, but not WAFTI. Oh no, not WAFTI! Somehow they felt that they would be able to maintain operations without disruption. I find this funny because WAFTI can barely maintain operations when all conditions are perfect, let alone when one of the biggest storms of the century is about to take place. I guess it must be the denial factor. Regardless, when I called central scheduling they informed me that there were no cancellations and my flight would be leaving on time Monday at 6:00 A.M. His exact words were, "It's just a

little rain"—tell that to the National Guard! The following is my
account of WAFTI flight 666 bound for Cleveland from New
York, LaGuardia Airport, that Monday morning at 6:00 A.M.

7:30 P.M. Sunday evening: Central scheduling informs me that
my trip will operate as scheduled and I am to report to
LaGuardia at 5:00 A.M. I begin to pray that the storm will escalate between now and then, forcing them to cancel flight 666. I
have dinner and get ready to go to bed early because in order to
be there by 5:00 A.M., I figure I'll have to get up at 3:30 A.M. and
hope to God I can hail a cab! I hold on to the thought that they
may call me within the next few hours and tell me to forget the
whole thing. Hope springs eternal.

9:00 P.M. Sunday evening: No call from central scheduling. I go
to bed listening to the freezing rain pelting against my window.

2:00 A.M. Monday: The phone rings and I shoot out of bed like
a bullet, thinking to myself, "It has to be canceled!" Sure enough,
it is central scheduling. "Is it canceled?" I ask, assuming that it
is. "No, you're still going," he said with malicious pleasure.
"We're just calling to tell you of a change on the second leg from
Cleveland to Chicago. It's leaving two hours later."

   Gee, thanks for waking me up to tell me. Couldn't they just
give me that information once I arrive at the airport? No, they have
to call in the middle of what is already a short night to inform
me. Between the end of that phone call and the wake-up time of
3:30 A.M., I toss and turn and try to fall asleep again without any
success.

4:00 A.M. Monday: I'm dressed and out the door. It's cold and
dark and I'm not happy. I hail a cab and tell the driver I'm going to

LaGuardia. He laughs at me. Real funny, pal. The ride is treacher-ous, but there really isn't a lot of traffic to contend with, so we arrive safely. When I pay the man his fare, he laughs at me again. Ha ha. As I suspected the place is deserted—granted it is about 4:30 in the morning, but this type of tranquility is highly irregular, even for that hour of the day. I notice on the flight display monitor that the other airlines have canceled all their flights; when I look at WAFTI's monitor it states that all their flights are on time. Well, since I'm here I might as well go along with the little charade.

I march on through security and down to the flight attendant check-in office. Everyone is there and feeling about the same way I am. We can't decide if WAFTI is the stupidest airline in the world or if they are making a smart move by not following the other airlines' lead. Maybe we will come out ahead by helping people get out of here instead of canceling everything. We also figure that since there are no other airlines operating this will be one day when there won't be a never-ending line on the taxi way for takeoff. In fact, we'll probably be able to get right out! After briefing with the captain, who, I might add, is also in a rather surly mood, we board the aircraft. It appears we will have only twenty-five passengers to Cleveland and it also appears that the heat's not working. I inform the captain that we are freezing our asses off in the cabin, and he explains that the APU is not work-ing. What exactly is the APU you might ask? It's the auxiliary power unit. What the hell is that? I don't really know, but it needs to be working in order to start the engines—and the heater. This is not a big deal, you just have to use an electric power cart to get the engines started and then once you push back, you're fine. However, until the engines are started there is no heat.

6:10 A.M. **Monday:** The twenty-five passengers have boarded, and all are asking for blankets. Fortunately, because the load is so light, we have enough for everyone. We're sitting at the gate with the door closed, attached to the electric power cart and waiting for a tug to push us back from the gate so we can get the engines started. Since we're about the only plane around, one would think it would be a relatively quick procedure for the tug to come over and push us back and get everything in motion. But for some reason we are not moving. We are just sitting there in what has now turned into freezing rain. It's so cold that I have turned on all the ovens in the back galley and opened them to get a bit of heat circulating. All the passengers and flight attendants are wearing their coats.

6:30 A.M.: Still waiting. It seems the tug we are waiting for has no chains on its tires and therefore cannot get enough traction to push us back from the gate. Someone on the ground is currently searching for chains or another tug. After what seems a long time the captain announces that they have located another tug. Thank God for small miracles. The tug appears to be working because I can feel a backward motion—we are on our way to the deicing pad. Deicing is a very important safety procedure involving a truck that comes out and sprays deicing fluid on the outside of the aircraft to prevent ice from building up on the wings, which adds weight and could affect the takeoff. Timing is very important when it comes to deicing because if the plane doesn't get off the ground in a certain amount of time (about five minutes) after it is accomplished, the ice will start to accumulate again and the whole procedure will have to be repeated. The best way to guarantee a successful deicing mission is to use two trucks, one on each side, right before the plane is ready to take off. This way there is no opportunity for ice to begin to build up again. I'm not joking about the importance of deicing, but when I began my career there was no such thing as deicing—someone just took a broom and wiped off the snow and ice from the wings and that was it. Today a great deal of money is spent on the deicing operation; the deicing fluid costs more than jet fuel. In any case, WAFTI has three deicing trucks at LaGuardia so one would assume they could deice the plane in a timely manner and send us safely on our way. Well, on this day, as luck would have it, one truck was broken and one truck was out of fluid. That left us one good truck and we had to wait for it. It was working overtime since it was the only available truck and WAFTI had another flight that was trying to get out ahead of ours.

7:15 A.M.: It was finally our turn and the truck came and began the deicing procedure. There was a light freezing rain outside, and freezing temperatures inside as we still had no heat and were basically relying on the ovens, coats, and blankets. Unfortunately, the deicing process took longer than normal because we had only one truck, so by the time the left side was finished and the right side was being worked on, ice and snow began accumulating again on the left. It was ridiculous. After all, for the previous three days all anyone was hearing about was the big storm, so you'd think they would have the deicing program up and running and maybe even a backup plan in place, but no.

8:00 A.M.: Finally the deicing has been accomplished, the engines have been started, and we're ready to get in line for takeoff. The weather outside shows no signs of improvement, but at least the cabin temperature has warmed up and people are more comfortable.

8:10 A.M.: The captain makes the following announcement: "Ladies and gentlemen, we very much appreciate your patience this morning with all our delays. I know you very much want to go to Cleveland, but as we were about to take off a warning light sounded in the cockpit. We feel it's in your best interests to have our mechanics take a look at the problem, so we will be going back to the gate. I'm sorry for the inconvenience, but your safety is our primary concern."

8:15 A.M.: We arrive back at the gate, but now the jet way is frozen and they cannot bring it up to the aircraft door.

8:20 A.M.: Somehow they get the door open and the agent comes on and makes the following announcement: "Ladies and gentlemen, we are sorry to report that flight 666 has been canceled. We do have another flight right next door at gate 4B that is leaving for Cleveland in ten minutes. Please take all your personal belongings with you and go next door and take any open seat. We will transfer all your checked bags. Thank you for your cooperation."

All the passengers rushed off. The captain came back and informed us that scheduling had called and we were all released from duty for that day, but we were to call them and they would give us new assignments for the following day to make up for the lost time. I certainly was looking forward to that. I said to the captain as I was leaving, "Well at least all the passengers will get to go to Cleveland today."

"I don't think so," he replied.

"What do you mean?"

"Well, keep it under your hat, but according to the manager out here, the entire airport has just run out of deicing fluid. No one is going anywhere, for now."

With that he went his way, probably back to his hotel to wait for a new set of orders, and I went mine, home to my cozy apartment to watch the falling snow.

Medical Emergencies

THE FLIGHT ATTENDANT profession has its roots in nursing. The very first flight attendants, or stewardesses, were required to be nurses. I guess this was because they found many original stewardesses from the military and most women in the military at that time (the late 1930s) were nurses. Although the requirements have changed over the years, the element of caring for people still lingers. Flight attendants care for and serve people of all nationalities, while traveling all over the world. We're trained in everything from CPR to comforting a fearful passenger, and more recently we've been trained on the defibrillator in the event someone has a heart attack on the airplane. And although it is not an everyday occurrence, serious medical emergencies on board an aircraft are not as uncommon as you might think, and when they happen it is very frightening.

I will always remember my first medical emergency. I had just strapped into my jumpseat at the back of the aircraft. I was seated next to another flight attendant and we were chatting as the plane was taking off. Before we had even reached a level cruising altitude we heard the call button ring, and I said to the other flight attendant, "It's not even safe to get up yet and someone is already bugging us. They probably want a glass of water." Then I heard another ring and then about three more. I turned to look out into the cabin and I saw about ten worried faces looking at me, motioning me to come over. I knew something was very wrong, because when they want a glass of water they have a completely different look on their faces. This was obviously something serious. I jumped up and ran to the epicenter, where I discovered a young woman traveling alone who was having a seizure. All the other passengers were scared and, to tell you the truth, so was I. I told my colleague to page for a doctor and let the cockpit know what was happening in case we needed to make an emergency landing. At this point, the woman began to come around and I asked her her name, and if she needed anything. She was able to tell me her name and we had a little conversation; she also wanted a glass of orange juice. It turns out she had never had any sort of seizure before and that she was going to visit some friends by herself. She said she felt a lot better and didn't want to have any medical personnel meet the flight, nor did she want a wheelchair. So we simply kept an eye on her the rest of the flight.

Some medical emergencies are not quite so simple and require more involvement. For example, there is the story of a flight attendant who was working a flight from somewhere in Asia bound for somewhere in America. The 747 was completely full. There were about eight hours until landing, when a man came up to the flight attendant and said, "My father is ninety years old and speaks only Chinese, but he is in a lot of pain because he has not urinated in more than fourteen hours." Apparently, the elderly man had suffered some type of prostate problem a few weeks prior, but had felt well enough to make the sixteen-hour flight. The flight attendant paged for a doctor and two responded, one Chinese woman and one Canadian man. They examined the man in the galley and asked the flight attendant if she had any medical equipment on board. Well, ladies and gentlemen, most major airlines now have terrific medical equipment on board, so if you should ever find yourself in the unfortunate position of being ill on an aircraft, you can rest assured that we have various machines and a full supply of wonderful drugs to see you through it. In any case, the flight attendant brought them the supplies and they rifled through the kit and found what they were looking for—a catheter! (I told you we have a lot of stuff.)

It seems that the doctors agreed that the gentleman needed to have a catheter inserted as soon as possible. The flight attendant had been helping the doctors, but she decided this might not really be her area of expertise. The doctors thought the best place to perform the procedure would be in the lavatory near the galley, so the flight attendant cordoned off the area with curtains, giving them as much privacy as possible. The two doctors and the elderly passenger went into the lavatory that was to function as an operating room. A few minutes into it the Canadian doctor was complaining to the flight attendant that he needed a lubricant and the supply kit did not include any. The resourceful flight attendant responded, "I have some Vaseline in my bag that I use to remove my eye makeup. If that would help you are welcome to use it." The doctor was thrilled and accepted her kind offer. A bit later the flight attendant was still assisting while simultaneously setting up the galley for the next service when the doctor called out, "I need something to drain the fluid into." The flight attendant was a bit perplexed by this one and was looking around when the doctor shouted, "Give me that coffeepot!"

The flight attendant dumped the coffee, quickly handed him the empty coffeepot, and when he was finished he handed it back to her. Then he told her to bring him some pillows and blankets. She left the galley (and the coffeepot) unattended while she went to search for the pillows and blankets in the dark, crowded cabin. When she returned she noticed that the cof-feepot was missing, and she assumed that the doctor was using it again until she noticed that one of her coworkers was out in the aisle about to begin a coffee and tea service—with the dreaded coffeepot. "Hey, Jonathan!" she screamed from the galley to the back of the plane. "STOP—DO NOT SERVE THAT COF-FEE!" Luckily he had not started to serve anyone, and he returned to the galley and that was the end of that coffeepot!

It's not only flight attendants who assist in medical emergen-cies; often pilots are called on to help because they also receive medical training. Recently, I met Captain Al, who told me a fas-cinating tale of a flight he had been on a few years ago. It seems that Al was a passenger on a flight from Los Angeles to Tampa, where he was living at the time. About midway through the flight, right around the time they serve the ice cream sundaes and cookies in first class, the flight attendant made an announce-ment: "Ladies and gentlemen, if there is a doctor or any other medical personnel on board this evening, please identify yourself to a flight attendant." A few minutes later Captain Al informed the flight attendant, who was running back and forth between the back of the aircraft and the cockpit, that he was an off-duty captain and if he could help in any way he would be happy to assist.

"Have you ever delivered a baby?"

"Well, I can't say that I have," he responded.

"Okay, would you like to try? Because there's a woman in the back row who is eight months pregnant and her baby is on the way into the world as we speak. There's no doctor, but there is a nurse who's helping us."

Captain Al pushed away his hot fudge sundae, set down his *USA Today,* and made his way to the back of the aircraft. Once there he discovered the young woman who was in labor. The nurse and the flight attendant had cleared away the other passengers and set up a makeshift delivery room in the last row. The woman was propped up against a big pile of pillows, and blankets hung from the overhead bin to serve as a curtain. The nurse was coaching her and directing another flight attendant when Al came on the scene.

"Hi, I'm Al and I am an off-duty captain. I have had some medical training and I thought I might be able to help you back here," he said.

"Thank you, Al. My name is Mary and I'm a registered nurse. This lady is going to deliver a baby very soon and I would welcome your help. She's at about ten centimeters and her contractions are about two minutes apart. If there's any way they can land the plane I would highly recommend it."

Al got on the interphone to the cockpit and explained what was happening to the working pilots. He suggested they declare an emergency and divert the flight. The working captain said that was already in progress and they were hoping to be on the ground within thirty minutes.

Al returned to the back row, where things had begun to escalate. Mary was repeating over and over, "Breathe, breathe . . . keep taking deep breaths." The plane felt as though it was beginning its initial descent when all of a sudden the patient's water broke and her pain seemed to increase.

Nurse Mary said, "Her contractions are now less than two minutes apart. Please make sure there is medical personnel meeting the flight and tell those pilots to hurry and get this plane on the ground!"

The plane was descending fast. Al was holding the woman's hand and trying to reassure her, telling her that they would be on the ground very soon. "Hey, I think I see the head coming. Does that mean she is going to have the baby right now?" shouted Al.

"No, that means she is going to walk around for the next three weeks with a head between her legs. Of course she's going to have the baby!"

"Okay, what should I do?"

"Just let it happen and I'll give you some basic instructions along the way," the nurse answered. The woman was screaming and the baby was on its way as the plane touched down. Moments later the paramedics were running down the aisle with all their equipment. There was some shuffling around before they decided it was best not to try to move the passenger because she was about to deliver the child at any second. Al stepped aside and within about five minutes you could hear the cries of the newborn baby girl. Captain Al was now positioned at the interphone and in contact with the working crew in the cockpit, giving them a play-by-play. When it was determined that the delivery was successful and all was well with mother and child, the captain made the following announcement: "Ladies and gentlemen, flight 1222 left Los Angeles with one hundred and twenty-five passengers aboard and we are pleased to report that we now have one hundred and twenty-six passengers aboard. Please welcome our newest passenger to the flight and to the world!" And with that everyone in the cabin broke into applause. Once mother and daughter were deemed stable to transport, they were safely removed from the aircraft. The new mother was alone in a strange city (since they had been diverted) and she was pretty scared so Captain Al agreed to accompany her to the hospital and catch a later flight to Tampa. Upon their arrival everyone at the hospital assumed that Al was the proud father! Once they cleared up that matter the woman asked Al to call her parents. He took the number and was delighted to make the call: "Hi, you don't know me. My name is Al, and you're not going to believe this, but . . ." Keep up the good work, Al.

The End of Summer

A FTER LIVING IN Greenwich Village for twelve months, Bitsy and I found a bigger, more comfortable apartment on the Upper West Side. It was a summer sublet and we had the place to ourselves until the leaseholder returned in the fall. He was an actor out on a national tour of some Broadway show. Things were going OK but Bitsy was getting tired of New York. One day she informed me that when the sublet was up in the fall she was going to move back to the Midwest.

"Moving back to the Midwest! What, are you nuts?"

"I'm over New York. Dragging my bag around on the subway, rushing to catch the Carey bus, paying outrageous rent for a dumpy apartment . . . present circumstances excluded. I mean for the rent we've paid over the years we could each have a home with a yard," Bitsy said.

"Who wants a home with a yard? Then you'd have to mow the lawn and shovel the driveway."

"I've made up my mind. I've been out here longer than you anyway. You'll see, one day you'll just wake up and want out!"

I tried to talk her out of it, but to no avail. She had, indeed, made up her mind and that was the end of it. We decided to have a fun summer, throw a few parties (the place had a big deck and a grill), invite some friends out from back home, and do all the New York things we had always intended to do, but never really got around to doing: the Circle Line boat tour, Ellis Island, Coney Island, the Bronx Zoo, and Le Cirque. We managed to do all of the above except for Le Cirque—we made it there, but only as far as the bathroom. Nonetheless we said it counted as having been there, so we could officially tell people we had been to Le Cirque. Of course, we still had to fly our trips and such, but we made a lot of time for having fun in the wonderful city of New York. Knowing that Bitsy, my longtime roommate and flying buddy, was leaving was not easy to digest. I felt a sense of impending doom and I knew my days were numbered. Soon I would have to find a new living situation and a new roommate . . . unthinkable! If I ended up living with someone who was a nine-to-fiver, they would be home every night and probably on the weekends. Too much togetherness, if you know what I mean. If I found another flight attendant, it would probably be a new hire who would be on reserve status, coming and going at all hours of the day and night. Most likely she/he wouldn't have any money and would probably screw me on the phone bill. I kept hoping there would be a last-minute change of heart on Bitsy's part, but when October rolled around Bitsy was gone. I decided to try finding my own apartment and living alone. This was a big adjustment, but I wasn't ready to leave the Big Apple yet. I began looking for places to live and trying to get the money together to prepare for the many costs associated with moving in Manhattan. After a long search I found a little studio on 102nd Street and West End. The apartment wasn't exactly great . . . I thought about jumping out the window a lot, but the place didn't have any windows. It did, however, have a dishwasher (a rarity in Manhattan, at least among my class). But I missed Bitsy and all the good times. I was depressed. My long-distance bill skyrocketed, and then I was even more depressed. To combat my depression I ran the dishwasher. It was comforting in a strange way. I also decided to get serious about my acting career. It was time to move forward!

Anonymous Confessions

I WANT TO LET YOU in on a little secret. Contrary to popular belief, flight attendants are not perfect. Most of us are pretty close to it, but occasionally we stray. I recently interviewed several flight attendants from different international airlines and asked them to confess to a wrongdoing. Here is a partial list:

I served a roll that fell on the floor.

I neglected to serve the chocolate-covered strawberries, and fed them to the flight attendants instead.

I told a passenger that she was going to make her connection when I knew damn well she wouldn't, just to get her off my back.

I've ignored passenger call lights . . . repeatedly.

I've served decaf coffee to the entire cabin instead of regular coffee, hoping they would all fall asleep.

I've walked down the aisle avoiding eye contact with passengers after the captain announced the flight had been canceled.

I ate the hard-boiled eggs off the Cobb salad in first class.

I told the first officer I would meet him for dinner and
then never showed.

When we ran out of bottled water I refilled the bottle with
tap water and served it.

I used my bare hands to put ice in the glasses.

I blocked off the back bathroom on a full 747 so that it
would be available for crew only.

When a passenger asked me for a pillow I told him I
would look and bring him one if I could find one, but
never bothered to even look.

I went into the first-class coat closet, found the adorable
man in 2B's jacket, and put a love note in his pocket.
(He later called me.)

I took an empty wheelchair from another airline near our
gates and "borrowed" it for one of our passengers who
had been waiting twenty minutes for a chair and had
to make a connection.

I inadvertently took home the passports of two unaccom-
panied minors from China and their return tickets
home. Instead of calling the company and reporting
my error, I called the place where the children were
staying (with their grandparents) directly. They came
over to my apartment the next day to retrieve them.

A passenger wrote a bad letter about a fellow crew member and asked me to turn it in to the complaint
department; I promised I would and promptly ripped
it up and threw it away.

I used my cell phone on the jumpseat in the back galley
when we were not supposed to use them.

I forgot to arm both back doors on the 757 and realized it
about an hour into the flight. I didn't say anything to
anyone else and quietly armed them when no one was
around.

I told a passenger it was my first trip when I had been flying for ten years.

On Trash

ONE OF THE THINGS I've become very well acquainted with over the last sixteen years is trash. I've been picking it up, stowing it, looking through it for lost objects, smelling it, seeing it, trying to find space for it, and saying "thank you" when people give it to me (a very humbling experience). Before becoming a flight attendant I never gave it a thought. But now I regard it quite differently than the average person does. I've even become interested in it and think about it on my days away from the airplane. I've watched the New York Sanitation Department with envy because they have that big truck in which to dispose of the Big Apple's wretched refuse. I wish we had something like that on the plane! We do have a trash cart, but it is nowhere near the sophistication level of the New York Sanitation Department. I mean, that truck can smash all the garbage with a big machine so there is room for even more garbage. When *we* need to make room for more garbage on the plane, we have to use a paper plate or some other device and manually shove it down with our hands to create more space. Pretty gross, especially for a person like myself who has a germ phobia.

Most flight attendants who've been flying for any length of time have probably had the unique experience of looking through the garbage for a lost article. One day in the early stages of my career I walked into the galley to find a very senior flight attendant rooting through the garbage. Appalled, I asked, "What are you doing?"

"Looking for the glamour that is supposedly part of this job," she replied bitterly. It was then that I realized how intimate my relationship with trash would someday be. I'm not alone with the trash, though. No, a great many flight attendants have shared their trash sentiments with me. We've had lengthy discussions on the subject. Some of the remarkable things we've found in the trash or things that have been given to us to kindly discard include:

Airsick bags
Diapers
False teeth
Eyeglasses
Panties
Paper cups full of used chewing tobacco (otherwise
    known as the Styrofoam spittoon)
Used condoms
Depends

We have also noticed that a person's rubbish can reveal a lot about his or her personality. Think about it: Flight attendants have the rare chance to not only notice what people throw away, but also the opportunity to observe the manner in which they throw it away. Here are some of the different personality types.

THE UTTER SLOB: They are heedless and unthinking when it comes to trash. These are usually the same people who are under the mistaken impression that all the overhead bins belong to them. When we tell them it's time to turn off their laptops they think that they are exempt because they're above everyone else. They are completely self-absorbed. Who do they think is going to pick up that newspaper, dirty pile of Kleenex, soda can, candy wrapper, and all the other little unmentionables they leave behind? Do you think they live like that at home? And it's not as if we haven't provided them with an opportunity to get rid of their unwanted items. We flight attendants come through the cabin fifty times offering to collect the trash. In fact, we beg for garbage! "Can I take your trash? Please? Oh, please let me take that for you! It would really mean a great deal to me if you'd give me your garbage. . . . Thank you sooo much!" I have gone up and down the aisle twenty times asking for garbage, and yet when all the people have deplaned the place still looks like it has been hit by a cyclone. Whatever happened to the idea of leaving a place better than when you found it? Or at least as you found it. I mean when you sat down in that seat three hours ago you didn't find newspapers, ripped-up documents in the seat pocket, and empty soda cans at your feet. Now, if you think I'm exaggerating just talk to the people who clean the planes between flight segments. I'm sure they have tales to tell.

THE TRASH SNOB: There is also a lot to be learned about people from the way they hand over their garbage. Some people give it to us as if they are the Queen of England and you are their humble servant. They can't look up from their reading material or be disturbed in any way with such a measly task as passing you their dirty tray. They completely ignore you and can't be bothered to pick up the tray from the table and pass it to you. No, you have to reach across two other passengers to get it and, of course, they can never say "thank you" because whatever the hell they're reading is simply too important to acknowledge your service.

THE ANAL RETENTIVE: Some people are very organized in presenting their trays to you. They take the time to put everything into a very neat, concise order. The other day I noticed someone who put all the flatware from his row into his empty tomato juice can. Very creative indeed, except that I had to remove it from the can in which it was wedged. Still, I appreciated his effort.

THE IMPATIENT TRASH GIVER: Some folks do not have the patience to politely wait for us to come and collect the trays. They don't want to have to stare at their dirty dishes, and because they just cannot wait, they put their trays on the floor. I understand this because I'm not a patient person myself. However, when flight attendants finally do come to collect the trays, please have the common courtesy to pick up the tray from the floor and hand it to the flight attendant. After all, when we served you we didn't serve you on the floor, did we? Thank you in advance for your kind cooperation.

THE EAGER BEAVER: Now, some people are so excited and eager to help out that they have their trash ready to go almost as soon as they've taken the last bite of that fine meal. Then they're smiling and waving that garbage at us from row seventeen, never mind that we are only at row ten. I guess they just want you to know that they're ready and waiting. We'll be there in a moment, Jethro.

THE BEFUDDLED TRAVELER: These poor folks are sort of baffled by the whole experience. They are not quite sure of how to get everything back onto the tray from which it came. They are aware that when it was presented to them it was in some sort of formation, but aye, how to return it to that formation . . . there's the rub! Instead of making an effort to do so, it's easier for this type of individual to just pile everything on top of the tray in a discombobulated fashion and quickly pass it to the flight attendant. Generally, they're very nervous, make little eye contact (probably out of embarrassment more than anything else), and sometimes their hands are shaking. They are usually the ones who spill the entire pile of food and trash onto the person sitting next to them and onto the floor.

THE LATECOMER: I guess these people are just slow eaters. You walk by them over and over and over again and they are still playing around with their peas or their cereal or whatever slop you just served them. The amount of food they have in front of them never seems to diminish. Although they appear to be finished, when you inquire as to whether you might take their trays out of the way for them, they just smile and say, "Oh no, I am still working on it." What I want to know is, what is it they're working on? They're certainly not working on eating it. Are they watching the effects of the altitude on freeze-dried food? Are they performing some sort of scientific experiment? Eventually they'll either summon the flight attendant or get up out of their seats and bring the trays to the galley themselves. This is usually right before landing when everything is put away and then you have to find someplace to shove the tray at the last minute. One time I had a man who refused to give up his food and we were about to land.

"Sir, I'm sorry, but I really have to take that now."

"But I'm not finished."

"Well, it's an FAA rule. I really need to take it."

"OK. Then can I take it to go?"

"Sure you can take it to go," I said, and without missing a beat, I picked up his tray in my left hand and grabbed an airsick bag with my right hand. I then proceeded to dump the leftovers into the bag and politely gave it to him. "Here, sir, is your doggie bag. Now fasten your seat belt, we're about to land!"

Dramatis Personae

THIS BOOK WOULDN'T BE complete without examining all aspects of the airline experience. So far, I've covered a great deal of material and I hope, gentle reader, that it has been enlightening. However, I have neglected to address an extremely important component, and that is the flight attendant. Oh yes, I've discussed them, described them, and included them in my tales. But in order for you to truly appreciate them and to understand the modern-day flight attendant, I must classify them. Besides, passengers and pilots can't always be the butt of the joke. And so in the interest of fairness and a thorough, unbiased account, I offer you now a carefully detailed study, an étude, if you will, of THE FLIGHT ATTENDANT. Please bear in mind, flight attendants are a very diverse group of people. In a sense they defy category. There's not a typical flight attendant, per se, but there are certain recognizable personalities.

Let us begin with a classic, THE COCKPIT QUEEN. She has been around since the beginning of time and will most likely remain with us until the bitter end. Does she want to meet a pilot? Does she want to find a husband? Does she want to find someone else's husband, or is she merely interested in aviation from a technical standpoint? The answers vary. I, myself, have spent a considerable amount of time in the flight deck, but that is because it's the only place where I can find solace from the unspeakable horrors of the crowded cabin. It's the only place on the plane, aside from the bathroom (which always has a long waiting line), that has a lock on the door. It is quiet and calm in the cockpit. The pilots are usually glad to have a visitor. The view is nice, and so is the change of scenery. For most of us it's a pleasant diversion, but not for the Cockpit Queen. Oh no, it is her home base. She's chomping at the bit to get up there and, once she does, you're not going to see her for a while. Everyone else will be preparing for the coffee and tea service, and the Cockpit Queen will be strangely absent. An inquiring mind will wonder aloud, "Hey, where the hell is she? I haven't seen her in forty-five minutes."

"Take a guess," another will respond.

"Again? God, with all the time she spends up there she should be able to fly a plane."

"She's not up there because she's interested in flying."

When you finally go up there to remind her that she has a job to do in the back, you will find her smiling and laughing, having a grand ol' time.

"Hey, it's time for the next service," you boldly announce.

"Already? Have I been up here that long? Time just 'flies' when you are having fun . . . ha ha ha hee hee . . ." Everyone laughs uproariously, as if it were the funniest thing they had ever heard. Then she follows you out of the cockpit, apologizing.

A harmless creature, but she can get on your nerves.

DRAMA QUEEN: Drama Queen can be male or female, it matters not. The most important thing here is that this character has a well-developed flair for the dramatic. And if there is no drama that day, Drama Queen has the ability to create some. Because a day without drama is a day without sunshine! And there's so much trauma in the drama. Whenever you run into this individual there's some major deal happening, and tension is in the air. She's flitting around, whispering things to other crew members. When you ask her what is going on, she raises her eyebrows, looks directly into your eyes, and says, very dramatically, "Nothing." The Drama Queen loves to instigate trouble, and will stop at nothing to have a buzz going on around her. If she can't dig up enough scandal from her own life she will dig some up from someone else's life. One thing is for sure—it will not be a dull flight if Drama Queen is aboard.

LOVE THE PERKS, HATE THE JOB: They usually have at least ten years seniority and can hold a regular schedule, but you can find brand-new people who feel this way also. They really don't give a damn about the job. They see it as a necessary evil, a means to an end. They need a paycheck and the benefits are nice, but the real draw is all the time off. They don't even necessarily like people or traveling. They fly the minimum amount of trips, do the minimum amount of work on the trips, and see their jobs with the airlines as a little break from their real passion in life. This "real passion" could be any number of things: real estate, going back to school, owning a small business, and my favorite of course, performing! Oh yes, so many stars in the sky. These folks are always begging you to come to their latest show. They're always droning on and on about how well their other career in the theater, film, or music business is progressing. If it's progressing so well, then why are they marching up and down the aisle collecting trash? To tell the truth, the performer's commitment to his "real passion" is admirable. I recently flew with a "jazz man" who was telling me about how he combined his music with his flying. It was really quite amazing. I mean, the guy was on reserve and yet he was playing gigs all over the world. He used his free travel benefits to get to the gigs and sometimes he would trade his trips so he could play a gig on his layover! He told me that he once worked a flight to Cairo and then ran to the hotel, changed his clothes, and took a taxi to some club where he was sitting in with the band. The following day he had to work a flight back to London. Another popular moonlighting profession is the salesperson. This individual is always selling something that he bought in bulk on his last trip to Hong Kong, Peru, or Macedonia. He often displays his goods on the layover and then offers them to the crew for purchase.

THE KNOW-IT-ALL: The Know-it-all believes he is right and you are wrong even if he is wrong. If he happens to be wrong, he will say, "OK, well it should be this way." These flight attendants are a real drag. They feel it's their duty to share with you all the information they have, and to hear them tell it, they have plenty.

"You're setting up the beverage cart incorrectly! We're supposed to do it this way."

"You didn't heat the meals at the proper temperature."

"Your shoes don't have a high enough heel."

"You better top off the ice."

They are like little police officers, and if not kept in check they can mature into THE DRILL SARGEANT. Whereas the Know-it-all usually confines her corrections to flight attendants, the Drill Sargeant goes one step further: she throws it onto the passengers.

"Raise your tray table *now*!"

"You will fasten your seat belt this very minute."

"Take your seat right now, sir."

"Stop interfering with my duties."

The core problem seems to be control/power issues. They must not have any control or power in other aspects of their lives, and since they have a little bit of authority on the airplane, they take it to the limit whenever possible. Now these people can be the nicest people once they get off the airplane. It's just that on the airplane this evil twin emerges and wants to take over the world. They think they're just doing their job, but in all reality they are making it difficult for everyone else on board.

THE SOUR APPLE: Everyone is entitled to a bad day, but these people are always having bad days. Being miserable makes them happy, and they aren't completely happy unless everyone else is miserable right along with them. You could give them a million dollars and they would still be miserable. There they are baring their teeth, growling about life. Everything sucks! The job sucks, the company sucks, life sucks, and when you're working with this type of flight attendant you're going to hear about it to the last detail. "The lights are too bright, the cabin is too hot, we don't get paid enough, this hotel is a dump, this crew meal is awful, I hate this captain, these passengers are annoying the hell out of me"—and that's within the first five minutes of meeting them. And for me, the Queen of Bad Moods, to comment on this, you know it has to be pretty severe. I have a lot of respect for bad moods, but this is beyond a bad mood. I think the best way to deal with this kind of person is to "steer clear." Too much negative energy.

THE PARTY GIRL: You gotta love this one! She's about twenty years old, and has maybe had a year or two of college, but it wasn't for her. She's not really the "studious type," as she will tell you, and one look at her will tell you that is no understatement. You might see her in the elevator of a hotel with a bottle of champagne in her hand, a shit-eating grin on her face, and sometimes a lampshade on her head. This chick has one goal in life and that's to have a good time. There's not a serious bone in her body, and no matter how close she comes to trouble, it never quite gets his hands around her. She always lands on her feet and never gets caught. Actually, her enthusiasm is contagious and she's fun to fly with because wherever she goes there's something going on! She has boundless energy, and she can stay out all night and still be there at 6:00 A.M. for pickup with a smile on her face. She lives for the layover, and on the airplane she practically joins the passengers for the cocktail service. You can take the girl out of Hooters, but you can't take Hooters out of the girl. One thing you want to avoid on the airplane is combining the Sour Apple with the Party Girl—this is not a good mix. Better to put Party Girl with Cockpit Queen.

THE OVERCOMPENSATOR: Male flight attendant. He comes on the airplane and wants to be sure everyone knows he's straight. The moment he meets you he gives you his bone-breaking handshake, but he's saying more than just hello. He's saying, "I'm straight. Straight as an arrow. Not all male flight attendants are gay! And don't forget it." In case it should slip your mind, the Overcompensator will periodically (like every five minutes) remind you of his sexual orientation. "My *wife/girlfriend* and I are going on vacation," "What kind of perfume is that? I think my *wife/girlfriend* wears it," or "Would you like to see a photo of my *wife/girlfriend*?" Any opportunity for him to work the term "wife/girlfriend" into the first thirty seconds of conversation will be exploited to the fullest. Lest you still have any doubt in your mind, he'll then begin discussing professional football, baseball, hockey, or anything else to do with sports. A dull subject in my opinion, but by God he's going to discuss it anyway—at length. Once you arrive at your final destination, he will never be seen walking through the airport with the other flight attendants, especially if there are any gay males on the crew. He walks ahead with the pilots.

Jumpseat Therapy

I N   A L L   Y O U R   M A N Y travels as a passenger on a commercial airliner, have you ever had the good fortune to be seated next to the galley where the flight attendant jumpseats are located? Oh, it's a real treat, I'll tell you! You don't need to shell out $5.00 for the audio/video programming. The entertainment next to the jumpseats is far better and much more stimulating than anything the airlines might offer you. While seated there, you're privy to all the galley gossip and assorted other little morsels that give you insight into the secret life of flight attendants. Flight attendants are often under the mistaken impression that when they've closed the galley curtain, no one can hear them. But voices do carry, especially when competing with a jet engine. Sometimes the jumpseats aren't even in the galley but in the cabin, and under those conditions you can really get an earful. If you are listening, you can learn a lot.

Usually flight attendants will be sitting in their jumpseats for takeoff and landing, and that's also where they eat their own meals after the service. Often they're engaged in conversation with other crew members. The thing you need to know about the nature of the flight attendant profession, gentle reader, is that quite often flight attendants have not necessarily met the other flight attendants with whom they are working on a particular trip. It's nothing like working in an office where you work with the same people day in and day out. In fact, when I go on a trip for work, I rarely work with the same crew members more than a few times a year. There's an ever-changing cast of characters. It gives the job a "stranger on the train" element. You feel you can completely open up and lay your burdens down at the feet of these total strangers because you'll never see them again. Here you are in Nashville on your way to San Francisco, and you're sitting about two inches away from a flight attendant you've never met before. The captain announces there's going to be a delay on the runway, but the flight attendants are to remain seated. Well, there you are, strapped in thigh to thigh with your new pal, good ol' what's her name. The two of you are in the galley jumpseat staring straight ahead at the ten meal carts two feet in front of you. Suddenly, she starts to cry.

"What's wrong, are you OK?"

"Oh, it's nothing. . . ."

You know it's something, but you try to be considerate of her need for privacy (rather hard to attain on an airplane) and respect her wishes not to discuss whatever might be the matter. After all, if she wasn't wearing a name tag, you would not even know her name. A few seconds later she starts to cry harder.

"Are you sure you're all right?"

"Oh, I'm sorry. It's just that . . ."

There could be a myriad of circumstances. Love-life problems, family problems, issues with other crew members on board, issues with passengers on board, problems with management, problems with medical bills, legal hassles, and so on. These topics in turn can lead to other topics, such as breast implants, birth control, fad diets, vacations, medications that relieve depression, medications that cause depression, exercise, how to invest in the stock market, teeth bleaching, gossip about other flight attendants, knitting, skiing, politics, Jesus, Chinese herbs, pilates, and transvestites—just to name a few.

"What is it? Do you want to talk about it?"

"Well, my brother-in-law skipped out on my sister and her ten kids. And then my sister split town with the man with whom she was having a love affair, and now I'm living in their trailer with the kids." She was sniffling a bit, but maintaining her composure.

"Gee, that sounds pretty rough."

"What?"

"I said that sounds pretty rough. I can see why you're upset."

"Oh, that's not the problem."

"What's wrong then?"

"I didn't get the Paris trip I wanted," she wailed.

There isn't a jumpseat big enough. Sometimes you need a couch!

In times of great desperation, I've also made a lot of "jumpseat confessions" to other flight attendants, some of whom I've never seen again. But these strangers carry some of my secret sorrows with them. This can be a very dangerous practice because even though there are thousands and thousands of flight attendants, it's a small world after all, and it's amazing how your confessions can come back to haunt you. My only hope is that my flight attendant confessors will keep their big mouths shut, should my name ever come up on the crew bus or in the briefing room. If they should share my secrets in a public place, those secrets are bound to become part of the rumor mill, and when that happens the first thing you'll discover is that the rumor mill has completely disregarded the facts and made the story more fascinating. From that point on, and probably to the end of your career, your reputation will precede you, which is very annoying if the reputation is a false one.

For instance, let's say you told someone that you were breaking up with your boyfriend because he was moving to another city and the two of you had decided that it wouldn't really work out, but there were no hard feelings and you have parted the best of friends. No drama. After the rumor mill gets hold of the story, the next time you walk into a flight and introduce yourself you will get the third degree from absolute strangers who have somehow heard about your ordeal.

"Hi, I'm Rene."

"Rene, Rene? . . . Are you based in New York?"

"Yes."

"Are you the one who was dating that guy? Wasn't he an alcoholic or something? Or was that someone else? Wait a second, I think that alcoholic thing is someone else. Anyway, didn't some guy dump you because he had another girlfriend and you walked in on them and discovered them in a very precarious position and then you threw a vase at him, which hit him on the head and then he threw a telephone at you, which hit you in the left shoulder, and now he is moving to another city and it was one of the worst breakups of your entire life? Weren't you guys engaged?"

"No, that's not quite correct. In fact, it's absolutely wrong."

"Well, honey, that's what they are saying about you around campus."

After you pick your jaw up off the floor, you run the risk of having the story completely twisted out of proportion and then spread around the airline. However, the rumor mill can also work in your favor. Let's say you lead a really dull life, but you don't want anyone to know just how dull. When you sit down on the jumpseat and start talking to your seatmate and they say, "So, tell me about yourself," you don't have to let on that you basically sit home every night, eating Lean Cuisine while watching reruns on Nick at Nite. Instead, you can embellish upon the facts of your life, or, if you choose, you can create an entire new identity for yourself. Of course, the problem with this is that you have to remember all the little (or big) lies you are telling about yourself so you don't get confused. I recommend keeping a little notebook in your flight bag.

Now there is the other side of the coin, which is, fortunately, far more common and that's the built-in support system that comes with the job. Misery loves company, and if you do have something you want to get off your chest, the jumpseat can be a great place to vent, even if you don't know your fellow flight attendant/therapist. Gets me through the flight. Most flight attendants seem to have an innate ability to listen, empathize, and usually give pretty good advice. I'm grateful to all my colleagues who have offered insightful counsel over the years. One day I was having a really bad time of it with a love-life problem. There I was sharing all the intimate details of my love relationship with a flight attendant I had never met before. Let's say her name was Helen. She was a lot older than I was, had been flying close to thirty years, and she was divorced. There we were on the jumpseats after the service: Helen was knitting and I was drinking a cup of horrible airplane coffee. The conversation went something like this:

"I'm so pissed off at my boyfriend," I confessed.

"What is the problem?" she replied.

"I don't know, I think he's a player. I don't trust him. At first, he was so great. Really romantic and attentive. But it's been only a few months and now he is really aloof and demanding. I think it is probably going to end soon. Another one bites the dust."

"They are all that way. What does he do?" Helen asked.

"I am almost embarrassed to say . . ."

"C'mon, what does he do?"

"He is a pilot. A captain, a rather senior captain."

"For us?"

"Yep," I answered.

"How long have you been flying, Rene?"

"Long enough to know better."

"Hey look, it happens." She didn't look up from her knitting. "Was he talking about marriage?"

"There was no official proposal, but he alluded to it. I kind of thought, Hey, if I did marry him, maybe I could quit flying and you know, do something else . . . like be an actress," I said.

"An actress? Let me give you a little piece of advice, Rene, husbands come and go, but there's always another cup of coffee that needs to be poured or some more trash that needs to be picked up. Even if you did get married, I'd hang on to the job. There are so many great benefits to it," Helen advised.

"Now you sound like my dad."

"All I'm saying is I've known a lot of flight attendants who get married two or even three times, but they never quit this job because they realize what a good thing it is. Their careers are more long lasting than their marriages. The ones who do quit usually regret it."

"Maybe you're right. This guy is really turning out to be a jerk. He thinks that just because I'm a flight attendant that I'm going to wait on him hand and foot at home."

"I was married to one like that," she said, and laughed. "He used to joke that he wanted me to wear my uniform around the house. Real funny. Underneath I think he was dead serious."

"You know, Joe jokes about that with me, too. Must be a pilot thing," I told her.

"They say that every joke has a little bit of seriousness in it. . . . Hey, did you say Joe was his name?" she inquired.

"Yes, Joe. . . . Why?"

"That's funny, my ex-husband's name is Joe. Did you say he's a captain?" She put her knitting down now.

"Yes . . ."

"For us, right?"

"Yes, he's a captain for us," I answered.

"Does this boyfriend of yours live in Dallas, on a ranch, by chance?"

"How did you know? Don't tell me . . ." I was getting a sinking feeling in the pit of my stomach. Helen obviously recognized the terror-stricken look on my face because she said, "Now, Rene, take it easy. I don't want to upset you, but is your boyfriend's last name Blow?"

"Yes, Joe Blow. That's his name."

"Well, Rene, meet wife number one. I did my time from 1971 to 1980, perhaps you've heard of me. Have you met the kids yet? I'm the mom."

"You're Rochelle's mom?" I asked incredulously.

"No, no, no. . . . That's wife number two! She is also a flight attendant. I'm the mother of Jim and Bill, they're older."

"Jim and Bill? I have never heard of them. I only know about Rochelle," I said.

"He may have forgotten about them. It was a long time ago." She went back to her knitting with a smile on her face.

"What about wife number three?"

"What about her?"

"Kids?"

"None that I know of. She was a flight attendant, though. She quit, so you don't have to worry about running into her, but number two is still flying and still in love with Joe. Very bitter, you know she wants him back, blah, blah, blah. So watch out for her."

I was stunned. "This is appalling! I can't believe you were actually married to Joe."

"Welcome to the family, honey. How about another cup of 'joe'?"

Modern-Day Air "Travail"

TRAVELING BY AIR these days is demoralizing. Let's admit it, the thrill is gone. I speak now on behalf of the tempest-tossed traveler, yearning to breathe free amid a sea of chaos, crowds, and confusion. Road warriors with travel savvy may have a better understanding of the system than vacation travelers who may venture out only once, maybe twice, a year, but even they have their moments of despair. Let us begin at the beginning, if for some reason you want, have, or need to go somewhere. It occurs to you that traveling by car, bus, or train might be better than going through the entire airline experience. You seriously consider these alternate modes of transportation only to realize that they are far too slow. You're in a hurry, need to get there now, you have things to do, people to see, history to make, and you can't be screwing around on some slowpoke train. Besides, you have acquired some "free mileage" from going into major debt on your credit card or by using your long distance excessively, so why not cash it in?

First of all, you have to buy a ticket. There are a plethora of ways to go about this: You can call your travel agent, check out the Internet, or, if you are very bold and daring, you can call your favorite airline directly! You make the call, then you're placed on hold for a long time with annoying background music underlying the latest details of their upcoming sale (this alternates with a well-modulated female voice breaking in to apologize for the lengthy wait). Finally the salesperson answers, and you tell her you want to purchase a ticket to XYZ and need to leave on such and such a date and return on such and such another date and you want the *cheapest fare*.

CALLER: What is the cheapest fare?
AGENT: Where are you starting?
CALLER: New York.
AGENT: Where are you going?
CALLER: Around the world.
AGENT: Can you be a little more specific? Like what is your first stop?
CALLER: Johannesburg.
AGENT: We don't fly there from New York, we would have to route you through Europe.
CALLER: I don't want to go to Europe first. Is there any other way?
AGENT: One moment please (she takes out her atlas). . . . Umm . . . you could start in Tokyo and work your way west.
CALLER: I don't have that much time.
AGENT: Perhaps you should call a travel agent and have them arrange a tour package for you.
CALLER: Call a travel agent? I AM A TRAVEL AGENT.
AGENT: One moment please.
Click.
CALLER: Hello, hello??

It's one of life's little mysteries how calls are conveniently disconnected when the conversation gets too complicated or too intense. Moving on, let's assume you have made a successful purchase. The next step is a trip to the airport of origin—what fun! If you can't get a ride from a friend or take a taxi then you have to drive your car. Big drag, because this will require *parking* your car. Sometimes it seems that the parking lots are bigger than the actual airport. Apparently most people go for the drive-yourself option because the parking lots are always very full. It also seems as if they're always under construction, so you end up having to park about one million miles away from the airport. But not to worry because the little courtesy van will chauffeur you from one of the lots to the airport. Of course, you may have to wait a while for it to arrive, and when it finally does you will then take a "see the airport" tour while the van picks up more and more and more people with more and more and more bags!

Eventually you will arrive at the airport, exhausted, just in time for the real fun to begin. These days most people do not check bags; they prefer to drag all their paraphernalia with them and hope that there is space for it in the overhead bins. However, if you should choose to check your bags you will need to proceed to the ticket counter where there is usually a long, long, long line of people standing, growing old, also waiting to check their bags and check in for their flights. It's interesting to me how technology is supposed to make things more efficient, and yet the more technologically advanced we become, the longer it takes to accomplish things. Don't worry, the line will move, it just moves slowly, so try and think of it as a chance to rest your weary bones from the car-parking experience. Finally it's your turn! You'll need to have that photo identification ready and you'll have to be prepared to answer a series of questions about your bags. Now if you find this annoying, just think about the poor agents; they have to ask every single passenger the same questions day in and day out: Did you pack your own bag? Has this bag been under your control since you packed it? (Actually, my bag gets a little out of control occasionally, but after I give it a good talking to it's able to compose itself.) Upon completely and successfully answering the twenty questions at the ticket counter, you're qualified to proceed to security. Another long line, a bit of radiation for the road, and you're off to the gates!

Congratulations, you've come a long way since parking the car. Your journey begins on the West Coast, you will make a connection somewhere in the middle of America, and then continue on to a major city on the East Coast. Let's also say that you're fortunate enough to have an on-time departure, an exit row, and your choice of a hot breakfast on the first leg of your journey. You think things are going well when you land on time in the middle of the country, but then it is time for that connection—this is where the trouble can begin. The plane lands, amazingly enough, *early*. Can't beat that; this is great because you had only about forty-five minutes to make your connection. This gives you a little extra time; maybe you will have a cup of coffee in the airport. You're waiting for the plane to park at the gate when suddenly the captain makes an announcement: "Ladies and gentlemen, the good news is we have arrived early. The bad news is they do not have a gate for us yet. It will be just a few moments while they locate a gate. Please remain seated, and thank you for your patience." Well, things could be worse. This isn't so bad. About ten minutes later, "Sorry folks, we're still waiting for a new gate, shouldn't be too much longer. Thanks again." Now you're beginning to get a bit concerned; at this point you're right on time and have exactly forty-five minutes to make your connection. Another five minutes pass and you feel the plane begin to move. It moves for a while and then stops. Apparently, they've found a gate . . . relief!

But what is this? No one is moving, and you begin to wonder, Now what? More waiting. You look at your watch and realize that now you have only thirty minutes to make that connection. What the hell is the deal, why isn't anyone moving? Another announcement, this time it's a flight attendant, "Ladies and gentlemen, we are having a little trouble with the jet way. Apparently they marshaled us in a little too far and now they can't open the door. They have to push the plane back a few feet, so please take your seats. Thank you."

Everyone sits down, sort of, and the aircraft moves. Then everyone rises again and after a brief pause the crowd slowly begins to inch forward. You're down to fifteen minutes' connection time, but at least you're off the plane and within the confines of an airport somewhere in the middle of America. From an architectural standpoint the place is a monument to stupidity—whoever designed it had no concept of the word "space." Having arrived at gate 99 you begin to walk in what you think is the right direction to get to gate 27; the place is crowded, kids are screaming, electric carts are beeping as they whiz past you, and all of a sudden you need to use the rest room. You locate one only to discover there's a line about a mile long . . . forget it! You still have about fifty gates to go when you discover you're walking in the wrong direction. Politely you try to navigate through the crowd, cursing the slower folks who are impeding your progress, tripping over baby carriages, and finagling your way through Japanese tour groups. You pick up the pace from a brisk walk to a jog, your heart is pounding, you're sweating, and everywhere you look there are people! Could this be hell?

Finally you get to gate 27 only to discover that your flight has been canceled. It's a mob scene at the podium. There are two agents, two computers, and two hundred disgruntled passengers of whom you are one. They're trying to rebook everyone on the next flight, and tempers are beginning to flare. After you catch your breath and compose yourself, you take your place in line, realizing you're at the mercy of the airline. It has been my experience that this is the most common time for air rage to kick in. You're up: "I need to get to XYZ today—do you think you can put me on the next flight at two-thirty?"

"That flight is oversold, you can be on the standby list, but there are already seventy-five people on the list."

"Well, when is the next flight after that?"

"Six o'clock. It's also full and there's also a standby list of about fifty people."

"Well, what do you suggest I do?"

"I can book you confirmed space on the ten o'clock flight tonight, which arrives at one A.M. at XYZ."

"It's about noon, so that is like ten hours from now. What am I supposed to do in the meantime?"

"Well, if you don't want to wait, I could reroute you through ABC at one and then you could catch the six o'clock from there, arriving in XYZ at eight, but you have to hurry and make up your mind because that flight is now boarding at gate eighty-eight."

Gate 88 is close to gate 99, where you just came from. The thought of rushing all the way back there is daunting. The other option is to sit and wait around for ten hours—what a choice. The pressure is mounting, there's a throng of people behind you, and the agent is impatiently eyeing you while waiting for your answer.

"Well, what's it going to be? I don't have all day." He may not have all day, but you might. You could take the next ten hours and think about all your options. . . . Maybe you should just go back home and forget the whole thing. You're practically ready to give up and then something hits you. You want to meet the challenge; a "yes, I can" attitude springs forth from somewhere in the depths of your soul. You think to yourself, I'm not going to let the system kill my adventurous spirit! You want to go where no man has gone before and you are without fear! You look the agent in the eye and boldly tell him, "Book me on the flight to ABC and call the gate. Tell them I am on my way from gate 27. I'm going to get to my final destination, even if it kills me, and nothing you or this airline can do is going to stop me." You take a deep breath, gather your courage, and begin to run through the airport to gate 88. This time, however, nothing can stand in your way. You shove through the crowds. You are unstoppable. An Olympic athlete of sorts, going for the gold. This is your parade and no one is going to rain on it. You arrive at gate 88, and the boarding area is empty except for the gate agent. She is waiting for you just as you commanded. . . .

"Hurry!" she yells.

"Out of my way!" you respond as you throw the boarding pass in her face and fly past her down the jet way and onto the airplane. At last you have made it, and what is this? They have given you a first-class seat! Life is full of pleasant little surprises, isn't it? Now this is more like it! An attentive flight attendant asks if she can hang up your coat or get you a drink. You give her your coat and ask for a glass of chardonnay as you settle into your seat. Granted, making a detour through ABC is not the most direct way to get to XYZ, but it sure as hell beats sitting around the airport all day. You've certainly made the right decision. You sip your wine as the flight attendant acquaints you with the safety features on board. Then a little word from the captain: "Ladies and gentlemen, hello and welcome aboard from the flight deck. The good news is that once we take off the weather is clear and it should be a smooth flight. The bad news is that we have a little mechanical problem and are going to be delayed indefinitely. Right now we're trying to locate another aircraft, so we want everyone to remain on board until we hear what the mechanics have to say. Thank you for your understanding."

You calmly wait. The chardonnay is easing your pain a bit,

and you're still better off than if you had chosen to wait around for another ten hours in the airport. The flight attendant comes around again for refills, this time with some warm honey-roasted pecans. Delightful! The captain interrupts your reverie with some wonderful news: "Looks like we have a new aircraft that's ready to go so we'll have you off to ABC before you know it. The only hitch is that we will have to transfer to a new gate. Please gather your personal belongings and proceed to gate 26. Thank you for your cooperation!"

After making the five-mile jaunt, for the third time in one day, you're now at gate 26. The plane is waiting, you board, the crew is there, it seems things are going to work out . . . but bad news. This time you don't have that first-class seat. This time you have a center seat—in coach. Things don't get much worse than that in life. It matters not, at least you have a seat on an aircraft that seems to be going in the general direction in which you want to travel. The door is closed, the safety demo is completed, and miracle of miracles, the plane is pushing away from the gate. Relief sets in, when all of a sudden the captain speaks: "Ladies and gentlemen, we're ready to go on our end, but the control center at ABC has informed us that a cloud is passing over ABC and the surrounding area, so they're holding all arrivals and departures in and out of ABC indefinitely. We're going over to a remote area and waiting for an assigned slot time. We'll be getting an update in forty-five minutes. In the meantime just sit back and relax, and we certainly do apologize for this inconvenience."

There you are, trapped on the tarmac because a cloud is passing over ABC. Not much to do but to think about the road not traveled. Perhaps you should have just hung around the airport and waited the ten hours for the nonstop to XYZ, which is where you really need to be. There probably isn't a cloud in the sky there, but you, genius that you are, chose to route yourself through ABC. Think how different your life would be if you had chosen the other alternative. You'd be in an airport with shops, restaurants, bathrooms, telephones, and Starbucks. But you picked this path. And now you're crammed into a center seat. On your right sits a three-hundred-pound bruiser who's taking a little catnap, shoes off and snoring up a storm, blocking easy access to the aisle, not a care in the world. To the right, by the window, sits a strange man from a strange land in strange garb emitting a strange odor from his body. He speaks in a foreign tongue, which is unrecognizable, yet you're becoming more and more familiar with it because he mutters constantly, with an occasional out-burst of sound that appears to have no defined meaning whatso-ever. Isn't this a cozy little arrangement? Well, you might as well get used to it because nothing seems to be moving. Sitting in the center seat is a bit like being in prison. You have no rights and you have no privileges; you are a nonentity.

Let's begin with the armrest. There are three seats, three people, but only four armrests. Guess what, center seat? You don't get an armrest! The man on the right assumes that both of the armrests are his, and discussion about the matter would be next to impossible because of the language barrier. The bruiser on the left is out for the count, and not only is he hogging both armrests with his burly arms, but his stomach is also drooping over what little area of the armrest remains, further invading your space. You've got the picture, I'm sure, because you're the unlucky victim of the "center seat dehumanization process." You will have to remain seated with your arms at your sides, facing straight ahead. What's a person in your position to do in the rare and unlikely event that you have the pressing need to leave your seat? Forget about it. You are not going anywhere, you are shack-led to the center seat. What do you need to get up and walk around for anyway, you little nonentity? When you were in first class on that last flight, you had some leverage, but since you have been relegated to coach class and to a center seat, your rights have gone out the window. It wouldn't be so bad if the passenger behind you wasn't a child who has discovered the joy of kicking the seat in front of him (yours), and he's screaming with delight each time he rams into you. You feel weary. Perhaps a nap would be appropriate, but alas, there is really nowhere to rest your weary head. You stare straight ahead, arms at your sides, head bobbing up and down, miserable. Finally it occurs to you: Maybe if you lower your tray table (you do have your very own tray table, that is one privilege you still retain) you could just lean forward and place your head there and close your eyes for a few moments and escape, if only mentally, the torture chamber, also know as the center seat. Yes, it works, and it's the first peaceful moment you have had in God knows how long. Just as you are about to fall into a deep sleep, the jerk in front of you decides to recline his seat back *all* the way, thus smashing your head so hard that it lands in your lap. Meanwhile the kicking from behind resumes, the muttering interspersed with occasional screams on the right continues, and the snoring on the left does not cease.

There you are curled up in a little ball, sucking your thumb, on the verge of uncontrollable sobbing, when the captain makes an announcement: "Ladies and gentlemen, I have some bad news. It appears we will be here for at least another hour. Please let us know if there's anything we can do to make you more comfortable. Thank you."

Heard It Through
the Grapevine

WHENEVER I TELL other airline employees I'm writing a book about our world, they all have wonderful little stories or jokes they think I should include. Of course, I can't mention them all, but here are a few goodies that I think you will enjoy!

There was a period of time when one airline was having problems with customs because flight attendants were bringing fruit from foreign countries into the United States and the airline was being fined each time it happened. So during flight attendant briefings the supervisors were reminding everyone not to bring fruit into the United States. One day a new supervisor at the base had to give the briefing. She was a bit of a scatterbrain and did not have a complete command of the English language. Her briefing went something like this: "OK everybody, listen to me. This airline been getting a lot of fine because flight attendant bringing in fruit from other country. Every time flight attendant bring in fruit this airline get fine. Bring in orange, one hundred dollars; bring in apple, one hundred dollars; bring in pear, one hundred dollars." At that point some wiseacre, unable to resist an opportunity to get in a little joke, raised his hand and asked, "What about grapes?" She answered, "That a good question. I check it out for you." She left the room, made a phone call, and then a few moments later came back and responded, "I check it out about the grapes and it is one hundred dollars per bunch, not one hundred dollars per grape. Thank you very much."

On a flight from A to B a flight attendant was serving meals. She had her airline identification badge attached to her belt on her skirt. At row 20, where the man in the aisle seat was asleep, she reached across to pass the meal tray to the passenger in the window seat and her belt and ID badge accidentally got caught in the sleeping man's hair, which, as fate would have it, was a toupee. He continued with his slumber and she with her meal service. The toupee, unbeknownst to her, was now attached to her belt. She realized it when a fellow flight attendant pointed out that she had a huge piece of hair hanging from her belt. Having no idea to whom it belonged, they had to walk through the cabin trying to find its rightful owner, but because he was asleep and unaware of his loss they were unable to identify him. When Sleeping Beauty finally awoke he came to the galley, rather wigged out, inquiring as to the whereabouts of his hair.

The weather was a bit rough and there was a lot of turbulence. Just before landing, a passenger rang the flight attendant call button:

F/A: Yes, may I help you?
PASSENGER: It's so turbulent. Do you think the captain will be able to land the plane?
F/A: I think so. We've never left a plane up here yet.

On a two-day layover in Chicago at the XYZ hotel, of which there are many and they all look alike, the entire crew went out for dinner. The senior flight attendant had been after the captain for years, and decided that tonight was the night she was going to make her big move. After all, they had the entire next day off in Chicago, so why not have a little fun? At dinner they had a few drinks, and she was flirting up a storm. Then everyone went out dancing and she was out on the dance floor with him the entire time. When the night was over everyone began to walk back to the XYZ hotel together, and by now the pilot and flight attendant were getting really cozy, holding hands, giggling, kissing . . . you know the drill. In any case, the lovebirds fell behind the others. The next morning the first officer was in the coffee shop having breakfast when the captain came in and joined him at the table.

"Hey, what happened with you two last night, everyone is curious. We looked back and you guys were nowhere to be found."

"Well, we got back to the hotel and went up to my room and the key didn't work, so then we went down to her room and her key didn't work either," the captain said.

"You're kidding. What did you do then?"

"We went to the front desk to complain and they informed us that we were at the wrong hotel!"

A female flight attendant was having difficulty with a disgruntled first-class passenger. She accidentally spilled a bit of bottled water on him while serving drinks on the ground during boarding. The passenger got really upset and said, "Jesus Christ, if you weren't so stupid you could do something else besides be a flight attendant."

A bit ruffled, she apologized and went into the galley to continue making drinks. A few moments later the agent came on board and made the final confirmation announcement, "Ladies and gentlemen, we would like to confirm that this is flight 123 to Washington, D.C., and thank you . . ."

Suddenly the disgruntled first-class passenger jumped up and said, "Washington, D.C.! I thought we were going to Miami. I'm on the wrong plane!" He then had to retrieve all his belongings and rush off the plane, thus delaying the departure. On his way out the flight attendant he had reprimanded earlier said, "If you weren't so stupid, you'd be able to get on the right airplane!"

On long international flights we turn off the lights after dinner so that it's dark in the cabin and people can sleep. About an hour and a half before landing we turn the lights back on and serve a beverage and a light snack. This also gives people an opportunity to wake up and prepare themselves for arrival. One day a passenger was so upset that the flight attendant had turned the lights on he could not contain his rage and screamed, "You turned on the lights when I was still sleeping. I can't believe you turned on the fucking lights!" The flight attendant, who was perky and alert (having been up all night), responded, "Oh no, sir, these are the 'breakfast' lights. You slept through the 'fucking' lights."

A very snooty lady handed her baby to a flight attendant. "Change my baby," she demanded.

"Excuse me?" the flight attendant responded.

"You heard me, change him."

"Change him?"

"Change him!" the passenger repeated.

With that the flight attendant went to the back of the plane and found another mother with a child about the same age and size, except this baby was a little girl instead of a little boy. She asked the mother if she would keep an eye on the little boy and if she could "borrow" her little girl for a few moments. The mother agreed and with that the flight attendant returned to the original mother and handed her the baby girl.

"What have you done with my baby?" screamed the outraged mother.

"You told me to change him, so I changed him," the flight attendant answered.

An aged little Indian man had been pushing the flight attendant call button above his head. You know the one I'm talking about—it has a little picture of a stick figure flight attendant wearing a skirt, and it's right next to the reading light. Anyway, this little old man had been pressing the flight attendant call button for quite some time, but no one responded. When someone finally did, he said, "What's going on? I've been fingering the flight attendant here for twenty minutes and she still hasn't come."

A passenger was having a little trouble opening the bathroom door, and the ever-helpful flight attendant responded, "Turn the handle—it's just like the one on your trailer."

The meal service had just commenced and there was some confusion as to where certain passengers who had ordered special meals were seated. The flight attendant made the following announcement: "Could passengers Smith, Jones, and Johnson please push your flight attendant call button." The flight attendant went out to straighten out the meal/seating problem. Upon arriving at row 22 the passenger said to her, "I'm the vegetable and my wife is the fruit." She took a good long look at him and responded, "Really? From the looks of it I'd say it was the other way around."

"Good morning, ladies and gentlemen! In a few moments we'll begin the breakfast service in the main cabin. We have a wide selection of choices for you today. You may have any or all of the following items: Prozac, Zoloft, Viagra, Ecstasy, Ritalin, Celebrex, or scrambled eggs. Some of these items may cause side effects, such as dry mouth, fatigue, internal bleeding, temporary blindness, and leprosy. Again, your choices include Prozac, Zoloft, Viagra, Ecstasy, Ritalin . . . oh, one moment please. My apologies, ladies and gentlemen, that is the *flight attendants'* breakfast menu. You passengers get the scrambled eggs!"

A passenger comes aboard with an upright bass. He has purchased a seat for the instrument because there is no place to stow something of that size and he didn't want to check it. He's having trouble getting it in the seat:

PASSENGER: Excuse me, flight attendant, can you come over here? I'm having trouble with my upright bass. What should I do?

F/A: I don't know, take up the flute?

Air Rage

Y OU'VE HEARD ABOUT IT, read about it, maybe witnessed it, or perhaps even been a victim of it. Apparently it's
getting worse and much more common. But what is air rage?
Basically it's like road rage only a lot worse because it occurs at
thirty-nine thousand feet and there are no outside resources to inter-
vene. In other words, you can't call 911. People are fed up with
delays, cancellations, overcrowded airports, and overcrowded
flights. They want the experience to be like it is on the commercials
and it's rarely that way. These days more and more people are traveling because the tickets are affordable and the world is getting
smaller. But the airports are having trouble handling the demand:
The air traffic control systems are antiquated and more runways are
needed, not to mention more parking spots, more gates, more first-
class seats, more pillows, more sodas, more wheelchairs, more people to push the wheelchairs, more magazines, more bathrooms in
the airports, more seats in the gate areas, more pay phones, more
personnel, more legroom, more room in the overhead bins, more
peanuts, more understanding, more attention, more instant gratification, more, more, more, more. But what they're getting is less, less,
less, and I personally think it's going to get worse before it gets better.

People on airplanes mirror society at large. On an airplane or
in an airport, on a bad day anyway, people are like rats in a cage.
They're at the end of their ropes—frustrated, angry, exhausted,

hungry, and pushed to their limits. How else can you explain some of the following things that have been occurring around the world recently?

1. Disruptive in-flight incidents have doubled in a twelve-month period.

2. Major airlines have decreased staffing by 5 percent; meanwhile, passenger loads have increased by 18 percent.

3. Incidents involving misconduct and abuse toward airline personnel have skyrocketed. Employee morale is low.

4. Recently, an enraged passenger heaved a suitcase at a customer service agent who was eight months pregnant.

5. A flight attendant was knocked to the ground and kicked after informing a hungry passenger that there were no extra sandwiches.

6. A man punched a pilot in the boarding area when he was informed that his flight was canceled.

7. A Saudi Arabian princess was sentenced and fined for choking a flight attendant.

8. After being denied a first-class upgrade, a passenger threw a full pot of coffee at a flight attendant, causing second-degree burns.

9. A passenger, angry about the lengthy delay, hurled a flight attendant into the lavatory door and attacked her until

restrained. The battered flight attendant crawled to the cockpit for help.

10. An intoxicated first-class passenger defecated on a meal cart during the flight.

11. An intoxicated passenger ignored the flight attendant's warning not to smoke in the lavatory. Cursing and demanding more liquor, the passenger reportedly smashed a bottle of vodka over her head. The flight attendant was severely injured and required stitches.

These are condensed versions of actual incidents. What's going on out there that could provoke such behavior? There are probably a lot of factors.

As I mentioned earlier, crowded conditions! You don't have to be a rocket scientist to know that crowded conditions bring out aggressive behavior. There's very little personal space in coach class on an airplane. I've heard the legroom is increasing, but even so it's still pretty miserable to be stuck in a center seat on a full flight for three hours. And the degree of an individual's misery is directly proportionate to the size of that individual— not to mention his personality, his expectations, what happened to him earlier that day, and most importantly, his relationship with his mother. You can't blame the airlines for wanting to sell every available seat. After all, they need to make money. But if they're going to pack passengers in like sardines it would be nice if the air-conditioning was working, especially in the summer.

Another contributing factor is alcohol! The longer some passengers wait, the more they drink. And with the delays these days that can mean a lot of drinking. They can be inebriated before we even have the chance to say, "Welcome aboard and we're sorry for everything we've done to you today." Airline personnel can deny boarding to intoxicated passengers, but often the boarding agent does not realize the extent of the problem. Once the plane is in the air, they might have another drink or two, which can put them over the top. Flying and drinking heavily do not mix (I know, I've tried it. Never on duty, of course). The effect of alcohol increases as the cabin pressure decreases. This can lead to some dangerous situations, particularly if you're over the ocean and someone who's drunk out of his mind decides he wants to get into something with the guy next to him, the flight attendant who just cut him off, or, worse yet, the captain.

We now come to a very interesting and common factor: sense of entitlement! This is when certain narcissistic features emerge: I'm a big shot and I deserve to be treated like one. These people feel that they're above everyone else, and their needs are more important than everyone else's as well. They're used to being doted on and having people shield them from difficult situations. Then they get on an airplane, where everyone suffers together and suddenly they're not so special. I mean, if the plane is delayed for three hours it's a delay for everyone, not just the folks in rows 15–45. These entitled people often can't handle the pressure of air travel as well as the common man. Personally, I think it's good for them to bear the pain with the rest of us. It builds character. Often they also have a problem with authority, as they're used to being in control and running the show. They can't fathom that someone, like a flight attendant who is beneath them in social status, would have the audacity to request that they shut off their laptops or cell phones or, God forbid, fasten their seat belts. These people, believe it or not, are often the ones who lose control on a plane, and argue with crew members about small issues that quickly escalate into larger, more serious problems.

One time, a very handsome middle-aged businessman got

really mad at me because there was no room for his three carry-on bags in the first-class overhead bins. Never mind that he boarded the plane about three minutes before departure. We were standing in the very front of the plane near the boarding door. I told him there might be space in the main cabin and asked another flight attendant to help him locate an empty bin because I was securing the galley so we could close the door as soon as his bags were properly stowed.

"I'm not putting my bags in coach. I'm a first-class passenger," he informed me.

"Well sir, we cannot leave until your bags are properly stowed. The other option would be to check them. I just offered the coach-class bin because most people don't like to check their luggage if they can have it on board instead. What difference does it make if it's in coach or first, as long as it's on the plane?"

"Because if I put them in coach I'll never be able to get back there to get them when the flight is over. I'll end up waiting until everyone else has deplaned before I get my bags. I do not have time to wait," he said curtly. I guess it didn't occur to him that he would have to wait at baggage claim with all the other common-ers if he chose to check the bags. I didn't bother to point it out.

"Sir, I really don't have time to discuss this. Do you want to find a place in the main cabin for your bags or do you want me to check them?"

His face got all red and he picked up his assortment of bags (which were way too big and too numerous in the first place), clutched them to his chest, and screamed, "CHECK THEM!"

With that he threw his luggage at me and stormed down the aisle to his seat. Luckily, I've had years of tap and I'm pretty fast on my feet. I moved out of the way before the bags hit me, but I think he smashed his computer because something made a bad sound when it hit the floor. Instead of making me angry, or hurting me, I thought it was funny because the guy really looked like an idiot. When people look like idiots it makes me laugh and that's just what I did—I started laughing! I didn't want him to see me laughing because I thought that might make him more angry, causing him to throw a pillow or a magazine at me, so I just went out to the jet way and checked his dumb-ass bags to LaGuardia. I thought about checking them somewhere else, like Fresno or Hong Kong, but my good judgment was still intact, so I decided to do the right thing. Besides, the guy was miserable enough. He slept the whole way to New York, so I didn't have any further interaction with him. When he was leaving I gave him my biggest, brightest flight attendant smile and said, "Thanks, have a great day!" In the interest of lessening potential air rage, I think this would be an excellent time to remind certain gentle readers, once again, that flight attendants are on board the aircraft to save your ass, not kiss it!

The mentally insane passenger can also be considered a disruptive passenger in the event that they get out of hand on the aircraft. Take, for example, this story: Bitsy was the senior flight attendant on a full 747 somewhere in Asia. The captain had informed everyone that there would be a bit of delay, perhaps as long as one hour, but the plane was going to push away from the gate and take its place in line. The plane slowly pulled back and seemed to go to a remote holding area and stopped, when suddenly a naked Chinese woman came running out of the lavatory. She was running up and down the aisles screaming in Chinese! Bitsy wasn't quite sure how to handle this because, although she'd had screaming passengers before and also naked passengers, she had never had a naked passenger who was also screaming. Aside from that, Bitsy doesn't speak a word of Chinese! Bitsy and a few others tried to catch the woman, but it's not really that easy to catch a naked person who's highly agitated and running around. They finally trapped her in the galley. It was there that she began swinging at anyone who came near her. Bitsy said that even though she was small, she could deliver quite a punch. Finally, she just collapsed and then urinated all over the galley floor. By this point someone had called the captain, who had returned the plane to the gate, where they were able to deliver the woman, now wrapped in a wool blanket, to agents meeting the aircraft. Fortunately for Bitsy, the plane was on the ground—not somewhere over the middle of the big pond where the problem could have escalated into something far worse.

I guess as long as the entitled, the intoxicated, the insane, and all the other people who can afford to purchase tickets are allowed to fly and the airlines continue to operate at over capacity levels amid a crumbling infrastructure, we'll have the potential for air rage. Now certain airlines are trying to teach flight crews how to handle aggressive behavior. Some are slapping the troublemakers with stiff fines and even jail time, and of course there's now something known as the Airline Passenger Bill of Rights. But I don't know what that means exactly and I don't think many passengers do either.

Tips for Travelers

I'VE ACCUMULATED A LOT of miles under my belt and now consider myself an expert when it comes to air travel. I've also consulted with other flight attendants in preparing this list of travel tips that will help make your journey more bearable:

TIPS FOR THE AIRPLANE

1. Lower your expectations. There is nothing glamorous or exciting about air travel. Expect the worst and hope for the best.

2. Try to book nonstop flights. If you do have to make a connection, allow plenty of time. More often than not flights are late, and even if yours is only a few minutes late, airports are so huge nowadays it can take thirty minutes to deplane and walk to your next departure gate. Give yourself extra time by creating a realistic connection. I would say at least three days—that way you don't have to rush.

3. Pack *one* carry-on bag that includes a bottle of water; something to eat, such as an apple, a bagel, or a candy bar; something to read; any medicines you may need; a toothbrush; a pen and paper; and any important documents that you don't

want to lose. If you're into electronic gadgets, you should also bring your cell phone, Walkman, and laptop on board with you—the rest of your belongings should be *checked*! There is not enough room on airplanes for everyone to bring two or three pieces of carry-on baggage. The rule should be one bag per person. The airlines are partly to blame for this one. Some airlines have one policy while others have another policy, so it's confusing. But something must be done because *the carry-on baggage situation is out of control!* People have boarded with hockey sticks, golf clubs, and copy machines. One man brought on the biggest box I've ever seen in my life and then asked me to help him stow it. When I asked him what was in it, he replied, "A toilet." He didn't think I was too funny when I informed him that we had four toilets on board that he was welcome to use. Am I crazy here or is trying to fit a toilet in the overhead bin a little much? If you don't trust the airlines to get your baggage to your final destination in one piece, ship it!

4. Things will go wrong; you can count on it. Your flight could be late, you could end up in a center seat, first class might be full, you might not get the meal of your choice, you might not get a meal, the flight attendant will possibly be in a bad mood, there might not be any good magazines on board, they might not hold your connecting flight for you, there could be a long line at the ticket counter. Don't take these things personally, and try not to get emotional about it! Yes, it sucks . . . big time. But look around you—everyone else is suffering, too. The airlines are not trying to deliberately ruin your life, although it may seem that way. I've had the same thought a number of times myself, but they're really not out to get you. In any event crying, cursing, barking, biting, and throwing things will not improve matters. I recommend yoga or a good muscle relaxant.

5. It's time for boarding. Try to go when they call your row number and not before. Not everyone can be seated in rows 23–35. Nor does everyone need special assistance or a little extra time for boarding the aircraft. Your seat will still be there and since you have checked all your bags you don't need to worry about overhead-bin space anymore.

6. You've made it onto the plane and located your seat. Now sit down in it! Lingering in the aisle only makes it more difficult for everyone else to board the aircraft. Also, if you think you might want a pillow and blanket during the flight, this is the opportune time to secure one for yourself. If you wait until everyone else comes on and fills up the bins with their bags, then all the pillows and blankets will be hidden behind the bags. It will be very difficult to find one later.

7. OK, when the captain or flight attendants make a request, please honor it. These requests are usually for your safety or for the safety of those around you. It isn't going to kill you to fasten your seat belt, turn off your laptop, put away your cell phone, or remain seated until the aircraft comes to a complete stop. Also, I'm sure you have seen it a million and one times, but as a courtesy to the flight attendants, could you put down your newspaper and at least *pretend* to be paying attention to the safety demonstration? And if you're talking, could you stop for two minutes? Maybe you aren't interested, but others seated near you might be. You may want to take a gander at the emergency placard located in the seat pocket in front of you. It takes two seconds and it might help you out in an emergency.

Tips for the Airport

1. Airports are crowded and massive. Fortunately, most of them now have what are known as "moving walkways." Here, ladies and gentlemen, is the universal procedure with these devices: If you're going to just stand there and watch the world go by, stand on the *right*. The *left* side is for the rest of us who are in a hurry, and need to pass. I repeat, if you are going to stand there like a bumbling idiot, stand on the *right side*.

2. When you're claiming your baggage—that is, if you took my kind advice and checked it—be sure you get your own bag. Many bags look alike. I speak from personal experience; I once took the wrong bag to my hotel room. Fortunately, it belonged to another crew member and we were able to straighten it out promptly—disaster averted. I also was on board when a passenger took a flight attendant's bag off the airplane in San Francisco. When the flight attendant realized she had someone else's bag (she figured it out by looking at the luggage tag on the outside of the bag), she correctly assumed this person had her bag. With a little help from the agent and the computer she was able to ascertain the woman's travel itinerary. She discovered the passenger was bound for Vietnam, so the poor flight attendant had to rush over to international departures and try to straighten out the mess with the passenger. And if you think that's easy, try taking a bag away from an old lady who does not speak a word of English and won't let go of her bag. All's well that ends well, though, and Suzy Flight Attendant was able to retrieve her bag and return the other bag to its rightful owner.

3. Stay out of the way of the electric cart. I'm sure you know what I'm talking about—the cart that's driven through the airport, incessantly beeping, pushing weary travelers to the edge of their sanity. Sometimes I think it has the same effect on the driver, because there have been instances when the cart has run down innocent bystanders. Traveler beware!

TIPS FOR THE HOTEL

You have finally arrived and you are now on the shuttle van to your hotel.

1. Wear your seat belt.

2. Tip the driver.

3. When you get to your room, don't use the telephone. This is one of those moments in life when a cell phone is a terrific thing. Hotel-room phones are a rip-off! What is a connection fee anyway?

4. Notice where the emergency exits are. One time Bitsy was on a layover and there was a fire in the middle of the night. The place was filled with smoke and she couldn't find her way in the hall. Instead she went to her window and crawled out onto her third-floor balcony, and from there a fireman helped her down. However, many hotel-room windows do not open, so that's not always an option. (And yes, she still had to work her flight the next day.)

5. If you're inclined to sit on that ugly comforter, make sure you're wearing sweatpants. Those things are filthy. I always recommend taking the thing off completely, or at least folding it over, so you can sit on the sheets. I know of someone who contracted a raging case of crabs and lice. He believes it was from the comforter—or else someone named Helmut. In any case, even though they say that they thoroughly clean hotel rooms, I always assume they're filthy. Better safe than sorry. I also wear thongs on my feet in the shower and I *never* take a bath in a layover hotel.

I hope you find these helpful and enlightening. . . . Bon voyage!

When Life Gives You Lemons, Make Lemonade

A S I MENTIONED EARLIER, after Bitsy left there was a void in my life, and I wanted to fill it by concentrating on my theatrical career. In theory this was a good plan, but in reality it wasn't that easy because I didn't really have a theatrical career! I was taking classes, going on auditions, and getting the occasional job here and there, but it wasn't very lucrative. Nor was it very satisfying. Then one night after a particularly rotten trip, I hit rock bottom. I was fed up with the fact that I wasn't getting any acting jobs and the airline job—no, the airline industry— seemed to be getting worse all the way around (I think this might have been the summer they let kids fly free). I didn't know how I was going to pull out of my bad mood. Maybe Bitsy was right, maybe it was time to throw in the towel and move back home. I was writing about my dilemma in my journal when all of a sudden, it hit me: This job is a treasure trove of material for a comedy, or maybe a tragedy! I could write my own play.

It was then that I decided I wasn't going to sit back and wait for Hollyweird or Broadway to discover me. I was going to go out and create my own thing. I decided to write my own show about my life as a flight attendant. Whenever I tell people I'm a flight attendant, they always ask a million questions. People must be interested in the subject! If no one would hire me as an actress, I'd hire myself! I didn't quite know what form it would take, but one thing was for sure . . . I was going to be the star. And so what if it was a flop? It couldn't be any worse than any other flop I had been in or had seen elsewhere. At least this would be *my* flop.

I put down my bottle of Jack Daniel's and started writing right then and there. And that's when my musical revue, *Around the World in a Bad Mood,* was born. I looked through my journal and came up with four little vignettes that very night. The next day on the airplane I started writing down ideas about everything I did and about every person on the plane. Suddenly all my horrible experiences had value and meaning! I continued working on it and within three months I had finished a script for a little one-hour show. I had some friends read it, which took a lot of courage, but they actually liked it. I began telling people about it and tried to assemble a team. I'd need a musical director, a director, actors, and a theater. How the hell was this going to all come together? I started by asking people I knew if they wanted to be part of my little venture: "Hey, I've written this little cabaret show about my job as a flight attendant and the airline industry. I'm trying to put it all together and I need

a _____

(fill in the blank).

Are you interested? I don't have a budget, but I'll be able to pay you something. What do you think?"

Here are some people's initial responses:

> "A show about flight attendants? Who is interested in that?"
> "No dough, no go!"
> "No, I don't think so. I'm busy until 2005 with my own
>   projects."
> "No."
> "I didn't know you could write."
> "No."

"I'd have to read it first."
"No."

And then finally, finally, finally, I heard someone say: "Yes, I'd love to be part of it. . . . When do we start?"

That was all I needed. I said "screw you" to all the people who said "NO" and went ahead and said "welcome aboard" to all those who said "yes." It went fast from there. I was so lucky to find all these talented people who were willing to take a chance and also have some fun. We rehearsed all summer, while I continued to fly, all the while accumulating new material.

The opening night was in September 1998, and it was fast approaching. I was passing out flyers like a crazy woman, writing press releases, and making a million phone calls a day to let people know about the show. And what really surprised me was how responsive people were to the idea—and not just airline personnel. It seemed that everyone had an airline horror story and thought the show sounded like fun. . . . Fun? Of course, I had very little money to actually pay people anything, so I ended up having to do a lot of the work myself, like writing lyrics for songs. I'd never done anything like that in my life, but Michael, my composer and musical director, said that I could probably do it. "Why don't you try?" he said. So I went home and tried. The first thing that came to mind was the safety demonstration that's done on every flight. I have that thing memorized, so just for the hell of it I tried to make it rhyme. Then I tried to make it funny. It was going pretty well until Michael told me it also had to fit into the music he had written, so back to square one. Finally, after a lot of blood, sweat, and tears, we came up with "The Safety Demo Shuffle."

I also did all the press work myself because I was in no position to hire a press agent. Fortunately, I was better at this type of work than I was at writing lyrics. I just wrote letters to all the newspapers and waited for them to get back to me. "Rene, don't hold your breath on these publications getting back to you," I was told. Or, "Don't be disappointed if you don't hear anything for a while. Like forever." But I figured, what the hell, it took five minutes to write the letter, so what if they throw it away. There's also the possibility that they might read the letter and be interested in the show. I knew I was on to something when the *Wall Street Journal* called and said they wanted to do a piece about it. They were the first of several newspapers to express interest and/or write a review.

Getting a show—any show—ready is a nerve-racking experience, but this just about put me over the edge. There were a lot of last minute changes and things to remember, and then there was this little voice inside that kept screaming, "You're going to FAIL!"

And then I would shout back, "I'm only going to do four shows and then I'm going to give up on show business. So I don't care if I FAIL! I'm still going to TRY!"

"FAIL."

"TRY."

"FAIL."

"TRY."

"FAIL, FAIL, FAIL FAAAAAAIILLLL!!!!"

"Places!"

As soon as I walked out onto that tiny postage-stamp-size stage, everything fell into place. Sure, there were weak points and some things that were awful. But there were some good moments, too, and the basic form was strong. People were laughing, and laughing, and laughing—granted, it was a kind and generous audience, full of friends, family, and flight attendants, but we were off and running. We're still running today! I hope it keeps going because writing and performing the show has been terrific therapy and I think it's made me a better flight attendant. So, as I like to say, when life gives you lemons, make lemonade!

The Job I Love to Hate

WHENEVER I GET GOING on one of my rants people often ask me, "Why don't you quit?" And do what? I mean, how would I pay all my bills and my rent? What else would I do where I have to work only twelve days a month and I can do whatever I want with the rest of my time? I mean, let's say I want to go to London to see the opening of a new play, or to go visit my best friend in Miami for a few days, or maybe take a trip to Africa. Now all I have to do is find a flight that has an open seat and I'm on my way.

When I began this flight attendant endeavor I was going to give it six months, maybe a year. Then I blinked my eyes and seventeen years had passed! I've invested so many years in it that I would be crazy to quit now. This is the type of job that improves with time. When you start out, you're at the bottom of the barrel and have to pay your dues by being on reserve, moving to a new base, earning low wages, and flying difficult trips. But as you move up the seniority list, your lot in life gradually improves. Suddenly you have five weeks' vacation, your salary increases, you can fly the kind of trips you like, bid the positions you like on the aircraft, and you can work your twelve days a month. You don't have to deal with office politics, and if you are working with someone you don't like, it's never really for more than a few days. After that, you may not see them again for another two years.

Ninety percent of the passengers are tolerable and the other ten percent you can easily avoid. You don't have to spend a fortune on office attire because you have your all-purpose uniform! So what if you have to wake up at 3:00 A.M. or stay up all night on occasion? So what if you have to pick up garbage all day long and perform other meaningless tasks? At least you don't have to take the garbage home with you. The moment you step off that airplane you're free, and that's a fine feeling. Besides, I'd be willing to bet that I'm not alone in having to perform meaningless tasks on the job.

This flight attendant job is more than just a job. It's a lifestyle that gets in your blood and, truth be told, it's hard to quit. It's sort of like golden handcuffs—even though you may want to leave, the benefits and lifestyle make it impossible to do so. That's why so many people stay with the job for thirty years or more.

I know a flight attendant who lives in Denver, gets her hair cut in New York, visits her parents once a month in Tampa, has a new boyfriend in Tulsa, and still has her teeth cleaned by her childhood dentist. Last time I ran into her I asked her how things were going and she replied, "I am *so* busy with everything I hardly have time to fly my work trips!" Some of the flight attendants who are mothers tell me they love to take their trips just so they can get away from the kids for a few days and enjoy the simple thrill of an uninterrupted bubble bath or room service.

Another flight attendant friend of mine, who has been flying for about five years, takes wonderful vacations. He has learned how to take his vacation, let's say for ten days, then manipulate his regular flying schedule so that he can add another ten days to it. Sometimes he can arrange ten to fifteen days off and that's without even using vacation time. Of course, he probably flies work trips back to back for ten days straight in order to have those long blocks of time to himself. He recently took a trip to

Thailand with another flight attendant, and he's also at work on assembling a collection of his photographs for a book he wants to have published. Some other places he went last year include Kenya, Prague, and Belize—not bad for a twenty-eight-year-old who probably earns about $30,000 a year. If he were working in the corporate world, he would probably make more money, but he'd never have the time to travel.

As for me, well, there is a certain splendor in being able to jet off for three or four days to Europe or Asia, or anywhere in the world for that matter, not knowing what will happen on the trip. The flight attendant job has also given me the inspiration to write my little musical comedy show, and you know that old saying, misery is the mother of all humor. If I were to leave the industry, where would I get my material, not to mention my audience? Aside from that, though, being a flight attendant has certainly influenced my personality. In addition to meeting and working with people from all around the world, being a flight attendant has given me an inner confidence. I mean, if I can successfully serve fourteen first-class passengers (usually businessmen) when there are only eleven meals on a flight that is two hours late and none of them are aware of the fact that I'm three meals short, I can do anything! I have also developed the patience of Job, probably from the millions of delays, misunderstandings about seat assignments, long lines, and having to wait for wheelchairs to meet the flight for our wheelchair passengers. I have also learned to work as a team member. When the weather is turbulent, and you have only two hours to serve a hot dinner, a complete cocktail service, and after-dinner coffee to two hundred people, everyone has to carry his or her weight. There's no time to discuss it . . . you just knock it out. I have also had the opportunity to witness human nature at its worst (no one willing to give up their aisle seat to an elderly woman with Alzheimer's traveling alone), and human nature at its best, which is usually something very simple (like the time we were short two meals and a woman and her child in the back row were not going to get anything except an apology and a bag of nuts, and the two people in the row in front of her offered to give up their meals). I've also had the good fortune to work in an industry where most of the other employees are terrific. For the most part they are fun, hardworking, honest, and make the difficult aspects of the job a lot easier to bear. I've always maintained that if you have a good crew, you can survive anything that may come your way.

Of all the traits I've developed from being a flight attendant, though, the most important would have to be humility. There is nothing like taking a walk down the aisle of an airplane a few hundred times a day asking people for their garbage and then saying "thank you" when they give it to you. I've also learned—and really believe—that there is a dignity in service, and sometimes in this disposable, instant-gratification-obsessed, self-absorbed society in which we live, it's easy to forget this. There's something intrinsically rewarding about helping a little old blind man to his seat, going out of your way to assist someone who is lost at Kennedy airport and who does not speak English, or taking care of a crying child who is traveling alone. I remember one woman whose husband had just died of a heart attack in the airport earlier that afternoon. She was on my flight later that day, on her way home to meet her children. She didn't want to sit in her seat so I invited her to sit on my jumpseat in first class and tried to comfort her during the flight while serving dinner to a full ship. When I see people with these kinds of problems I try to treat them as I hope others would treat my grandparents or my children if they were in the same situation. Grace under pressure, dignity, tolerance, and patience are some of my favorite qualities, and being a flight attendant has certainly helped me develop these qualities. So, when people inquire as to whether I plan to quit the job anytime soon, my answer is *no*. Because for all the mechanical delays, weather delays, oversold flights, canceled flights, early wake-ups, missed holidays, jet lag, sleep deprivation, antiquated air traffic control systems, lousy food, fleabag hotels, and unhappy travelers, it's still a great job. Besides, I've given this industry the best years of my life, so I'm also going to give them the worst. I'll fly until I drop . . . which might be soon!

AROUND THE WORLD IN A BAD MOOD

JFK to O'Hare, Fresno, Fargo, Eau Claire,
Memphis, L.A., down to Birmingham. . . .
All in day? Every step of the way.
Around the world in a bad mood!

Instead of seeing the world and all of its sights,
I'm picking up trash and breaking up fights.
Hoping to God there's some leftover booze.
Around the world in a bad mood!

Airports are crowded, the people are rude,
Lines never-ending, wear sensible shoes.
Carry-on baggage not worth what it weighs,
Oversold flights and weather delays.
(Those damn weather delays, sometimes they last for days.)
This ain't worth what it pays!
It was snowing all day, every flight was delayed,
I met a strange man bound for Amsterdam, we popped
Quaaludes, I woke up tattooed.
Around the world in a bad mood!

Where is the glamour? I gotta know where.
Times are a-changing up here in the air,
All of the clamor that can't be subdued.
Cheap, chintzy portions of horrible food
(I hate cheap chintzy food)
Do you have to be rude?
(Can't stand aeroplane food)
Puts me in a bad mood.
I got bumped off eight flights, I've been here three nights
Trying to get home from Timbuktu.
I slept on the floor, I can't take no more!
Around the world in a bad mood. . . .
Hoping to God I don't come unglued,
Around the world in a bad mood.
Whatever I do, I always get screwed.
Around the world in a bad, bad, bad mood!

Thanks, Buh-bye

W E ARE NOT AT the gate yet, so please remain seated with your carry-on bags stowed until I acknowledge some of the people who have made the show and the book possible.

This book is based on a musical comedy that I wrote in 1998 and I'm very grateful to the many people who have helped me with both. So beginning with the show I send heartfelt thank-yous to the following individuals: Michael McFrederick, my collaborator and the composer of all the fabulous music in the show, for encouraging me to write lyrics and keep going forward, and for his sense of humor. Tom Mills, for his fine direction and encouragement and also for his patience and understanding with a first-time writer who presented a lot of her material to him on airplane cocktail napkins. Collette Black and the terrific staff at Rose's Turn, for all their support and kindness to the cast and crew of *Around the World in a Bad Mood*. All of the talented actors and musicians who've made countless contributions and helped to bring the ideas, songs, and characters to life: Terry Dunn, Dana Fialco, Erik Hill, Erin Romero, Dave Horak, Suzanne Adams, Kerri Aldrich, Jennifer Winegarder, Hector Coris, Nicole Taylor, Julia Barnett, Woody Regan, Tracy Stark, John Flynn, Dan Chouinard, and especially Lou Rudy, who has been my calming influence and the best friend a girl could ever hope to have, for taking all the risks he has taken. Before *Bad Mood,* he had never appeared onstage, and now we can't get him off the stage!

Jennifer Bowles—Designer Extraordinare.

I am also very grateful to the journalists and other people in the media who have taken an interest and either written about the show or invited me on their programs to promote it. I know the show would never have gone on this long without the help of their interviews and articles, so thank you: Larry Zuckerman, Leslie Eaton, Edward Keating, Tim Russell, Kristin Tillotson, Jayne Clark, Joe Sharkey, Margo Adler, the BBC, *Minneapolis/St. Paul Magazine,* Simon Hirschfield, Tom Brokaw, Minnesota Public Radio.

With regard to the show my thank-you list would not be complete if I overlooked the importance of the help, guidance, and encouragement I have received from different theatrical associates. First of all, to Dean Seal and the Minnesota Fringe Festival—having the opportunity to play on the big stage at the Music Box Theatre in Minneapolis was such a wonderful, fun experience. Also, to all the people at Richard Frankel Productions/Scorpio Entertainment for their enthusiasm and their willingness to take a chance in developing the show and helping me take it to the next level.

Keep your seat belt on, I'm not quite finished! That was just the show, now on to the book!

I absolutely have to thank Jennifer Lang and everyone at Hyperion Books for all their support and interest. I still can't really believe I've written a book. Thank you for the golden opportunity.

I also have to thank my trusted legal advisors, beginning with Jason Baruch, who has helped me navigate the stormy sea of contracts, copyrights, and collaborator agreements. I'd be lost without you. Also, to Mr. Ernie Lindstrom and all the folks at the Lindstrom Law Offices who have been advising me over the years about so many things, but most recently about I'll Be Right Back Productions.

Of course, I thank all my longtime friends and my family for listening to me, putting up with my crazy antics and my wacky moods (it is probably jet lag), and supporting me in all my creative endeavors. Also, very special thanks to Patricia Bowles, Helen Jordan, K.O., Peter Spelke, Jon Austin, John Heenehan, Harold Spelke, and of course, O'Malley and Suzi.

Above all I want to especially thank the many flight attendants, pilots, and other airline personnel throughout the world who have shared their stories and experiences with me. I'm glad to be part of such a diverse, hardworking, fun group of people. I'm so grateful to the many of you who have come to the show and encouraged me to keep going and supported me on so many levels. This book is for you—happy landings!

For more information about the performance schedule of *Around the World in a Bad Mood*, call (212) 712-8702.

Author's Note

O N SEPTEMBER 11, 2001, I left LaGuardia Airport at
8:00 A.M. on what was to be a two-day trip to the West
Coast. About one hour into the flight the captain called
me into the cockpit. I unlocked the door and stepped in as I have
done a thousand times before; however, this particular visit was
unlike any other time before.

"Rene, we have an emergency situation. It seems that two
planes have been hijacked and have crashed into the World
Trade Center."

I couldn't comprehend what he was saying to me. I simply
could not believe it. "Do you mean there was a midair collision?"
I asked.

"No, I mean that two planes have been hijacked and deliberately crashed into the building."

At that point the voice of an air traffic controller came over
the cockpit radio, "The Pentagon has just been hit. Repeat,
another plane has just crashed into the Pentagon."

With that I sat down and felt my entire body go numb. I
must have looked awful because the captain asked if I was all
right. I said I was fine and waited quietly as the pilots took down
information about the revised flight plan.

"Rene, the FAA has declared a national emergency and all
aircraft have been ordered to land at the nearest airport. We have

been assigned to Green Bay. I'd like you to prepare the cabin. I don't want you to make any announcements regarding our rerouting until we are on the ground. We will be landing in fifteen minutes. Oh, and whatever you do, don't let anyone near the cockpit door."

Somehow I stood up, walked back into the cabin, and quietly informed the rest of the flight attendants what was happening, all the while trying to hide the fear I was feeling beneath a calm exterior. What happened after that is pretty much a blur. After we landed the captain made some brief announcement, and then the ground personnel took over. The passengers deplaned very quickly, and we were directed to the other side of security; within minutes the airport looked like a ghost town. We were instructed to go downstairs to aircraft operations and wait until we had new crew orders. When we arrived, there were many other rerouted crews already there, and for the next two hours we sat glued to a small television set in an employee break room watching the terrifying events unfold before us. Later the captain informed us that we were to go to a hotel and wait until we were released to go. We spent the next four days in Green Bay, Wisconsin, waiting, wondering, and watching. When we were finally released we took an empty airplane to New York, and as we flew into the city on approach we had our first glimpse of what is now called Ground Zero. Although we had witnessed the images for the last four days on a television screen, nothing could prepare us for the actual sight of the devastation of the horror below.

I finished writing this book on September 6, just five days before this tragedy. Since then the world has changed, New York has changed, and I guess I've changed, too. However, I still believe in humor and that laughter can help us heal. Although I did not personally know any of the flight crew members who lost their lives in the line of duty, I still feel a strong connection to them. They were, after all, sister and brother flight attendants, and to me they are also heroes just like the police officers, firefighters, EMTs, and countless other people who lost their lives while simply doing their job that day. Airline employees are an interesting bunch of people with a very interesting lifestyle; in our little community we are always sharing funny stories about our flights, our passengers, our coworkers, our layovers, and our lives. Needless to say, there is always a lot of laughter. Much of this book is not only from my own personal stories but from the collective experiences of all airline personnel, which is often what binds us together. And so this book is for all of us who travel by air and who work in the industry, but most especially for those we've lost.

September 24, 2001